The Joshua Ministry

God's Witnessing Army

by
Rev. David W. Hopewell, Sr.

Orman Press, Inc.
Lithonia, Georgia

The Joshua Ministry
God's Witnessing Army

by Rev. David W. Hopewell, Sr.

Unless otherwise noted, all Scripture quotations are taken from the HOLY BIBLE, KING JAMES VERSION. Scripture quotations marked NIV are taken from the HOLY BIBLE, NEW INTERNATIONAL VERSION. Copyright © 1973, 1978, 1984 by the Zondervan Publishing Corporation. Used by permission. Scripture quotations marked NKJV are taken from the HOLY BIBLE, NEW KING JAMES VERSION. Copyright © 1979, 1980, 1982 by Thomas Nelson, Inc. Used by permission. All rights reserved.

Copyright © 2001. All rights reserved. No part of this publication may be reproduced in any form or means without the prior written permission of the publisher.

ISBN: 1-891773-30-5

Printed in the United States of America

Orman Press
Lithonia, Georgia

Dedication

This book is dedicated to my wife Edie and our children, David Jr., D'Lisa, D'Juan, and D'Andr. I want to thank them for their support and prayers during the long hours spent working on this book.

I want to give special thanks to my wife for her support, prayers, and for working alongside me in the ministry. I thank God for a supportive family, not only in word, but they all help in the ministry and lead the personal life of a witness.

Acknowledgments

I first thank God for leading me to Greenforest Community Baptist Church in Decatur, Georgia, and for Pastor George O. McCalep. I thank God for a passion for lost and hurting people, and a passion to equip the believers to win the lost. I also thank God for the gifts, talents, and abilities He has given to me.

Further, I would like to thank Pastor McCalep for allowing me to exercise my God-given gifts and talents, and for trusting me in a leadership position by completely empowering me to develop and implement the Evangelism Ministry. I would also like to thank the members of Greenforest for their support and submission to my leadership in the Evangelism Ministry.

I am appreciative to Verba Johnson, Edward Smith, Tammy Rice, and Mildred McNair for their help in the editing process. Special thanks go to Rosalind Barnes for her suggestions, her editing, and for guiding me through the whole process. Special thanks to Sis. McCalep, Sarah Reid, and the entire Prayer Ministry at Greenforest for their long hours of prayer and support. God has truly blessed me to be around a special church with special people. To God is all the glory.

Table of Contents

Foreword 7

Introduction 8

Chapter I 11
        The Joshua Ministry Strategy
      Principles for Successful Evangelism

Chapter II 22
       Phase I —Members Helping Members
    Neighborhood Blitz • Ministry Opportunities

Chapter III 33
      Phase II — Churches Helping Churches
Unity of the Body • Existing Ministries • One-Year Strategy

Chapter IV 46
        Phase III—The Joshua Generation:
          God's Witnessing Army
Passed to the Next Generation • Teen Gospel Presentation

Chapter V 59
        Phase IV — Special Forces
  Pass Before Your Brethren • Reaching the Forgotten

Chapter VI **64**
Possessing the Promised Land
A Joint Effort • God's Part • Leadership's Part • Members' Part

Chapter VII **76**
Where Do We Begin?
Prayer

Chapter VIII **84**
Four Ts
Teaching • Training • Tally • Testimony

Chapter IX **103**
Tools in Our Hands (For Sharing the Gospel)
Love: The Ministry of Reconciliation • Personal Testimony • Invitation • Excitement • Prayer

Chapter X **115**
The Delivery System

Chapter XI **124**
Rewards of the Labor

Conclusion **128**

About the Author **129**

Foreword

The Joshua Ministry, written by Rev. David Hopewell, should be read by all Christians who are serious about carrying out the Great Commission. *The Joshua Ministry* challenges readers at every level to "keep the main thing (evangelism) the main thing." The book not only challenges, but it also instructs in a very simple way the "how-to" of evangelism.

The Joshua Ministry was birthed out of the passion for lost people that burns continually in the heart of the author, Rev. David Hopewell, Sr., *and* is based on a biblical principle couched in the Old Testament Book of Joshua. However, Rev. Hopewell has put flesh on this word in a model evangelism ministry that he has implemented at the Greenforest Community Baptist Church. The model stands on a testimony for the biblical principle *The Joshua Ministry* challenges us to utilize. *The Joshua Ministry* accepts the responsibility given in Matthew 28:19-20 without ignoring receipt of the power given in Acts 2.

In other words, *The Joshua Ministry* is based on an Old Testament principle that is incarnated in the marching orders of the Great Commission and empowered by the Holy Spirit. Read this book and adhere to its challenges, privileges, and instruction.

Introduction

The doors of our churches swing wide with parishioners seeking to worship the Lord in spirit and truth, but very few parishioners leave from those same doors and enter into the fields, which are ready for harvest. The question is—How can we experience God's presence during a powerful service filled with praise, worship, and a life-changing word, then leave out of those same doors of the church, get into our cars, and drive by fields ready to be harvested? Likewise, how can we go through our normal everyday routine allowing perhaps hundreds of persons to pass us by daily, but never once communicate the Gospel message to a lost friend, neighbor, loved one, or stranger? Does God's power only move us into a posture of praise and worship, but not into the field of harvest?

The presence of God experienced on the day of Pentecost in Acts 2 moved those who previously had been filled with fear into the field of harvest (instead of by the field). Of course, not all churches or members neglect the field. A small percentage actually does share the Gospel in the field on a consistent basis. However, this scenario of fields not being harvested describes a significant number of our churches today. The church exists for two reasons only: a) to edify or build up the saints through teaching and preaching and b) to evangelize. When choosing between building up the Body or evangelizing, most churches spend their time building up the Saints, with little or no evangelism. Since the primary purpose of the church is to evangelize, the most logical question is, Why is there either little or no evangelism in our churches today? Have we chosen to be disobedient to God? Have we no passion for lost and hurting people? I know that every church will have members who will choose not to evangelize; however, I don't believe that our pews are totally filled with saints who refuse to obey and fulfill the primary purpose of the church—to win the lost.

There may be many reasons why evangelism is almost nonexistent in many churches today. I have placed churches that don't evangelize in four primary categories: (1) *The untrained church*—these are churches that don't know what to do or how to do it; (2) *The fearful*—these are churches that have allowed fear to chain them to their pews. The grip of fear has them so locked up that their eyes have become blind to the lost and their ears closed to the cries; (3) *The sincere church*—these are churches that make a sincere attempt to evangelize, but lack strategy, structure, and accountability; and (4) *The uneducated church*—these churches believe that the call to evangelize is for the evangelist or a small group within the congregation, and not for them personally. However, regardless of the reasons churches don't evangelize, the call to evangelize the world must be answered by the entire body of Christ.

This book offers a strategy and principles rooted within the Book of Joshua that will provide steps to help churches create strong evangelism ministries and offer practical teachings to equip congregations of believers for effective evangelism work. The book will also identify those things that keep congregations chained to the pews and offer solutions to break those chains, so we can begin to move out and harvest the fields that await us.

I sincerely pray that those who have a need for the material in this book will recognize it and greatly benefit from it. I pray that God would raise up laborers to harvest the fields, so that lives will be changed, and that He will be glorified through our efforts.

Chapter 1
The Joshua Ministry Strategy

The Joshua Evangelism Ministry Strategy was given to me in prayer after accepting a ministry position at Greenforest Community Baptist Church in Decatur, Georgia, where the Reverend Dr. George O. McCalep, Jr. is senior pastor. The evangelism strategy and principles are based on several chapters in the Book of Joshua. These Scriptures give us a strategy for evangelism, and offer step-by-step principles for successfully possessing our land through evangelism. The Joshua Ministry Strategy is found in the first chapter of the Book of Joshua in the following Scriptures:

Strategy

> **But to the Reubenites, the Gadites and the half-tribe of Manasseh, Joshua said, "Remember the command that Moses the servant of the LORD gave you: "The LORD your God is giving you rest and has granted you this land." Your wives, your children and your livestock may stay in the land that Moses gave you east of the Jordan, but all your fighting men, fully armed, must cross over ahead of your brothers. You are to help your**

brothers until the LORD gives them rest, as he has done for you, and until they too have taken possession of the land that the LORD your God is giving them. After that, you may go back and occupy your own land, which Moses the servant of the LORD gave you east of the Jordan toward the sunrise. (Joshua 1:12-15, NIV)

Overall, the Scripture reference above brings the entire Body of Christ together on a consistent basis in the fields or neighborhoods of others. It professes that as members of the body of Christ, we must help each member evangelize, meet the needs of others, and help them possess their land. Just as Joshua reminded the brothers to cross over the Jordan to help their brothers possess their land, we, too, must cross over any obstacle to help our brothers possess (evangelize) their land (neighborhoods). The strategy will be looked at in depth in the next chapter.

Along with a strategy for evangelism, the Book of Joshua also provides tremendous principles to guarantee our success as we gather in the harvest.

Principles for Successful Evangelism

Spy the Land

"And Joshua the son of Nun sent out of Shittim two men to spy secretly, saying, Go view the land, even Jericho." (Joshua 2:1)

Notice in this chapter and in the eighth chapter, the land was spied upon before any attempt was made to possess it. Important information had to be gathered about the enemy so that an effective strategy could be developed to overcome the enemy. Likewise, before we try to possess the land or evangelize any neighborhood, we must first "spy the land." To "spy the land" means that we need to look at the demographics of the neighborhood. Furthermore, we need to learn the needs and problems of the community and know who is in the area (such as other agencies and faith-based organizations) because we may need their assistance to effectively minister to the needs of the people. We need to know the controlling spirits in the area. You must have knowledge of your enemy before you invade his territory. This information is very critical and needs to be given to your prayer ministry so they can effectively and strategically pray over the area and bind all hindering spirits. "Spying the land" is just good wisdom that will enable you to do a more effective job of ministering to the lost in the community.

Follow God's Direction

> "And they commanded the people, saying, When ye see the ark of the covenant of the LORD your God, and the priests the Levites bearing it, then ye shall remove from your place, and go after it. Yet there shall be a space between you and it, about two thousand cubits by measure: come not near unto it, that ye may know the

way by which ye must go: for ye have not passed this way heretofore. " (Joshua 3:3-4)

God gave Joshua specific directions on how to possess the land. In chapter six, specific direction was given on how to obtain Jericho. In chapter eight, in the taking of Ai specific direction was given. God may have a specific strategy to take the land and meet the needs in the community. He may have a certain part of the community in which to start your efforts. I have found that God will lead you to the right person, who is receptive and has a real need for ministry at that specific time. In most cases, another day or even another hour would be too late. If we don't get direction we could miss the move of God, so it's significant to get direction before we engage the community.

Sanctify Yourself

"And Joshua said unto the people, sanctify yourselves: for tomorrow the Lord will do wonders among you." (Joshua 3:5)

Along with "spying the land" and following God's direction, each member who evangelizes must sanctify him- or herself in order to effectively implement the Joshua Strategy. To sanctify means to be set apart or to set aside. It is a conscious decision to be sensitive to God's leading. It means to allow God and His gifts to flow through you to effectively minister to others. If we ever wonder why sometimes there seems to be an absence of God in our efforts, maybe it is because we haven't sanctified ourselves before God. Maybe there is sin in the camp. In chapter seven, Achan sinned by taking the accursed thing. As a result, God's presence in battle had taken leave. Without God, there was no way they could stand before the people of Ai. However, in chapter eight after the sin was put away, victory was assured as God revisited His people now cleansed from sin. Sanctification was the key to a successful encounter with the enemy. Likewise, if we sanctify ourselves, God will dwell in our presence.

Notice what Joshua said: "God will do wonders through you." Yes, you. God will use you not only to minister to someone through prayer and meeting his or her needs, but He will use you to do a miracle. To be used to transform a person from the kingdom of darkness to the kingdom of God is the greatest miracle in the world. Yes, God will and wants to partner with us to perform miracles. We must sanctify or set ourselves apart so that He can.

Move Out in Faith

> "And it shall come to pass, as soon as the soles of the feet of the priests that bear the ark of the Lord, the Lord of all the earth, shall rest in the waters of Jordan, that the waters of Jordan shall be cut off from the waters that come down from above; and they shall stand upon an heap." (Joshua 3:13)

Possessing the land was a huge assignment for the children of Israel. However, in order for God to manifest His power to assist them, they first had to move out in faith.

There always must be the element of faith in what we do for God. As long as the assignment seems too much and too overwhelming, then the glory for what God does will be His alone. When we realize our inability to accomplish what He has told us to do, we will then depend on Him for help. To sit around waiting on God to do something won't produce a manifestation of His power in our life. However, if we first move out at His command, without exception, He will always meet us and manifest Himself in our midst. We're not sitting around waiting on God; God is waiting on us. Those who carried the ark stepped out by faith and led the way. The ark represented God's visible presence with them. Today, this could be any Spirit-filled believer. They moved out in faith. Without faith, our efforts will only be our own. We must first move out in faith before God will manifest Himself in our efforts.

God Will Confirm His Presence

> **"And Joshua said, Hereby ye shall know that *the living God* is among you, and that He without fail will drive out the enemy." (Joshua 3:10a, emphasis added)**

As long as the people sanctified themselves and faith was present, God showed up and showed out. We will know that God is with us when lives are changed. We will also ascertain this by statements that come out of the mouths of those we minister to—statements such as, "I couldn't seem to get out of the house today," "I was out but had to come back home for some reason," "I have been praying for a church home." There will be confirmation of a divine appointment. God has always, in some way, confirmed His presence in our midst.

God Will Give You a Testimony

"That this may be a sign among you, that when your children ask their fathers in time to come, saying, What mean ye by these stones? Then ye shall answer them." (Joshua 4:6-7)

The testimony will be discussed later; however, if you reach out in the lives of others, God, without fail, will give you and them a testimony of His presence among you. There will be so much excitement in the lives of those that have been changed that they will begin to share their experience with you and others. Those used by God to make a difference in these persons lives will also be so charged up that they won't be able to keep it to themselves. God had given the people a testimony that was to be shared with others.

Give God the Glory

After the victory of Ai, Joshua built an altar to the Lord that had given them the victory. We must always give only God the glory. There is no way we can take credit for what He does in our midst. God deserves all the praise and all the glory. Let's be careful not to give the praise to anyone or anything, only Him.

The Joshua Ministry Strategy is an evangelism strategy that helps us possess our land and evangelize our neighborhoods. The strategy is a systematic strategy that brings consistency to your evangelism efforts. The strategy is unique in that it calls for all of us to take part in the fields or neighborhoods of others. The Joshua Ministry Strategy provides a strategy, basic principles, and basic evangelism teaching that will equip any church or Christian to do effective evangelism in the inner city, suburb, or rural area, thus helping them possess their land.

The Joshua Ministry Strategy has four phases, which will be discussed in this book:

1. Phase I — "Members Helping Members"
2. Phase II — "Churches Helping Churches"
3. Phase III — Teens, "The Joshua Generation: God's Witnessing Army"
4. Phase IV — "Special Forces"

These four Joshua Ministry phases will allow involvement of all members of the congregation, and equip them to engage in personal and door-to-door witnessing, reaching all persons regardless of social, financial, political, or ethical status. The effective use of these four phases will bring a complete evangelism arm to the church and bring organization and structure to its efforts.

The Joshua Ministry Strategy is not the only evangelism strategy, and is not designed to replace an existing effective evangelism ministry. The purpose of the strategy is to provide guidance for those seeking an effective strategy for their church or for those who want to help bring organization, structure, and consistency to their efforts.

Chapter 1 Questions

The Joshua Ministry Strategy

1. List the primary Scriptures on which the Joshua Ministry Strategy is based:

   _____

   _____

   _____

2. List the seven principles for successful evangelism:

   1. _____
   2. _____
   3. _____
   4. _____
   5. _____
   6. _____
   7. _____

3. List the four phases of the Joshua Ministry:

   1. _____

   2. _____

   3. _____

   4. _____

Chapter II

Joshua Ministry Phase I: Members Helping Members

In Joshua 1:12-15, Joshua repeats the words Moses had given to the tribes of Reuben, Gad, and half the tribe of Manasseh.

> "And to the Reubenites, and to the Gadites, and to half the tribe of Manasseh, spake Joshua, saying, Remember the word which Moses the servant of the Lord commanded you, saying, The Lord your God hath given you rest, and hath given you this land. Your wives, your little ones, and your cattle, shall remain in the land which Moses gave you on this side Jordan; but ye shall pass before your brethren armed, all the mighty men of valour, and help them; Until the Lord have given your brethren rest, as he hath given you, and they also have possessed the land which the Lord your God giveth them: then ye shall return unto the land of your possession, and enjoy it, which Moses the Lord's servant gave you on this side Jordan toward the sunrising."

Overall, this Scripture reference brings the entire membership and body of Christ together in the neighborhoods of others to help them possess their land through evangelism. It professes that as members of the body of Christ, we must help our brothers evangelize and meet needs in their field of harvest—their neighborhoods. The instructions were to leave their belongings, and help their brothers possess their land on the other side of the Jordan River (Num. 32:23). As we look at the Scripture reference in Joshua from above, we will discover two principles that can be used to help us in our evangelism efforts. These principles are *help* and *until*. Both of these principles help bring the consistency needed for a successful evangelism effort in our communities.

Help/Until

In verses 12-15, Joshua tells the people to "help" their brothers "until." The word *help* here suggests just that—to help. The word *until* suggests that the action can't be a one-time effort, but a continuous campaign. To be effective in our evangelism efforts, we must continually cultivate the soil or neighborhood. In chapter one, God promises to give them every place their feet touched. In chapter three, when they placed their feet in the Jordan, the river was given to them. They possessed it and its banks rolled back. However, we must be consistent. In chapter four, after taking their feet out of the water, the waters returned. This is a valuable lesson we must learn. Once we have put our feet on the land and begin to evangelize and meet needs, God's Spirit goes to work and change begins to take place. However, if we don't continue our efforts, the community and its residents will, just like the Jordan did, go back to their original state. We need to understand that a one-time effort of evangelism is not going to give us possession of the land. There are those who will not be at home, as well as other needs in the community that we may miss. The two words *help* and *until* convey both the prayer of Jesus for unity in John 17 and Paul's message of unity in the Body in 1 Corinthians 12.

The word *help* in verse 14 suggests not only leading the way or showing them what to do, but also getting in there with them! This was a sacrifice for Joshua and the people. They were to leave and help their brothers to possess their land until they had rest (vv. 14-15). These men were to help until their brothers were in possession, control, or could handle things themselves. Since they were more skilled in fighting than their brothers, they were to lead the way. To "go over armed before their brothers" meant they were suited up or prepared for the task. This suggests that ministries with expertise and resources in the area of evangelism should lead and help others that lack these skills. When God blesses us with more than enough, we should be willing to bless others. On the other hand, those who need help should not allow pride to stop them from receiving help from others. We are all one body, so we need to help each other possess our land.

The aid and support from their brothers wasn't a one-time deal, but a continued campaign. These men ate, slept, cried, grieved, and celebrated the victory together. I am not suggesting that we leave our families and everything we own and move into the homes of others. However, I am suggesting that we commit to helping each other achieve a more productive evangelism effort in our communities.

Possession on the east side of Jordan (Num. 32:33) was based on brothers helping their brothers possess land. The land of their possession on the west side of Jordan was a good land to raise cattle. However, these tribes were to lead the way and help their brothers possess their inheritance. Helping others evangelize and meet needs will help gather in the harvest, provide an opportunity to teach and train others, and allow others to leave the pews of their church to engage in the harvest fields of others.

Members Helping Members Possess Their Land

The evangelism strategy of "Members Helping Members" possess land is implemented through the Sunday School. Just as the passage of Scripture in Joshua 1:12-15, the Sunday School classes can be placed in tribes. The number of tribes can vary from one to twelve, based on the size of the Sunday School. This strategy was first implemented at Greenforest Community Baptist Church. Joshua told three tribes to go over to help their brothers; they were the tribes of Reuben, Gad, and half the tribe of Manasseh. Greenforest has fifty-one adult Sunday School classes, so a fourth tribe was added, the tribe of Ephraim (Joshua's tribe). This allowed there to be thirteen classes in each tribe. Each class has an *outreach leader* who is responsible for leading his or her class members in evangelism and thus meets the needs in every member's neighborhood. The goal of each class is to evangelize and to meet the natural needs of those living in the community. After completing these efforts in a neighborhood they move on to subsequent streets, helping members possess their land.

Before evangelizing a community, the first task is to "spy the land" (Joshua 2:1). It's important to get a sense of the people who live in the community, and their needs, and to determine what assignments will be given to each team.

Prior to going out into the community, an evangelism workshop is provided for those who have never been trained in the area of evangelism, while also sharpening or refreshing the skills of those who haven't been out in a while. Role-playing the testimony and Gospel presentation section of the seminar helps the participants to be more comfortable when they evangelize in the community. The workshop seminars empower and equip members with the ability and comfort to knock on doors and engage in personal evangelism.

The tactics of Phase One—"Members Helping Members" allow us to meet our neighbors' needs too.

As we knock on doors, sharing the Gospel, we try to meet as many needs as possible. If we see that we can't meet the need, we pray for that need because sometimes the only thing you can do is pray. Once that person's need is prayed for, it's easier to set the need on the sideline, allowing the door for sharing the Gospel to be opened.

Sometimes, in an apartment complex, the needs in the community can be found out from the management or others in the community. The tribe can become further involved in the community and meet needs by such activities as outdoor games, carnivals, mentoring programs, tutorial programs, baseball or basketball programs, outdoor concerts, health fares and more. The idea is to get involved in the lives of others by meeting needs. The kingdom of God is built on relationships. Since the most effective way to evangelize is through relationships, we build relationships through meeting needs or by getting involved in other ways such as those listed above.

Needs Met Through the Fivefold Ministry Purposes of the Church

The needs of the community are met through the fivefold ministry purposes of the church—*Evangelism, Discipleship, Missions, Ministry, and Fellowship.* As the Outreach Leader in the Sunday School class leads the class members into the field or neighborhood of the class members, evangelism most often takes place first. It is during this time of sharing the Gospel that needs surface. From here, class members will meet the needs through the fivefold ministry purposes of the church. The fivefold ministry purposes open the door for effective ministry. Door to door sharing the Gospel is *evangelism*. Meeting the needs of people is *ministry*. Being of the physical campus of the church makes it a *mission* project. Ongoing *discipleship* is taking place by new enrollments in Sunday School. Classes can have fellowship activities during the year, which should include the members of the neighborhood. This doesn't mean that every person in the neighborhood hears the Gospel message, but our goal is to present the Gospel message to at least one member in each family, and complete the other ministry purposes—missions, ministry, fellowship and discipleship. However, effective ministry cannot be achieved through evangelism only, but must address the entire man—spirit, soul, and body. If the members notice that a need can't be met through their efforts, then a referral may be necessary. The important thing is to meet the need. Remember, the lost person may be angry with God because of the present condition; therefore, we need to address the need because this gives us the best chance to have a listening ear for the Gospel. It's also good to know the other churches, faith-based organizations, and government agencies in the community, to assist in meeting the needs of the neighborhood.

One of the many ways that Greenforest Community Baptist Church helps meet needs has been through classes delivering food baskets at Thanksgiving. The classes adopt families, take toys to the children at Christmas, and meet other needs throughout the year. This is all made possible by the efforts and financial support of the class members. Financial support also comes from the church. The church tithes 10 percent of its budget to missions. This enables the church not only to evangelize, but also to minister to the natural needs of the person. As a result of these efforts, the Gospel has been shared, and ongoing ministry takes place. Residents from one apartment complex commented that members from Greenforest seem to be in their complex every week. Three managers from three different apartment communities have noticed and commented about the ongoing efforts of Greenforest members helping their residents. Just think of the kind of effect this kind of evangelism effort will have on someone in your community who has a need or a desire to attend church but needs that extra nudge. When one of your neighbors has a need or considers going to church, he or she will give the church that is visible in the community the greatest consideration. The needs in the community open to us a door for ministry that no other effort could.

Sure, some people are only after the fish and loaves; however, this must not stop our efforts to reach out to them. People did the same thing to Jesus. We need to understand that this is always a possibility when ministering to people who are hurting. We can learn something from Jesus here—He always met the need first. Once Jesus met the need, He got an audience. The door was wide open for additional ministry. Once we meet the natural needs of people, a door will open for us to share the Gospel to a more receptive heart. Those expecting to reap large numbers for their evangelism efforts will need to be patient. This process will not yield the big numbers at first. But the farmer who plants in hope knows that the one seed he plants will produce a greater harvest. This principle is found in the fourth chapter of Mark's Gospel:

> **A man scatters seed on the ground. Night and day, whether he sleeps or gets up, the seed sprouts and grows, though he does not know how. All by itself the soil produces grain —first the stalk, then the head, then the full kernel in the head. (vv. 26-28)**

We don't want to just throw our seed on the ground. A good crop takes time. If we just share Christ to a hard heart that may be closed to the Gospel, we will be just casting our seed. However, by meeting the need of the person, the soil of their heart will open to receive the Gospel. The fivefold ministry purposes of the church are one of the greatest ways to do effective ministry and close the back door of the church. With members helping members, together church members touch people where they hurt, and meet them at the point of their need. Our communities will never be possessed if we never leave the walls of our churches and are not consistently entering the field of harvest, sharing Christ and meeting needs. It takes time to grow a harvest or to win a soul to Christ. A continued effort of evangelism, discipleship, fellowship, ministry, and meeting the needs of the total man, will produce a healthy, stable harvest in our community.

Chapter II Questions

The Joshua Ministry Phase II — Members Helping Members

1. What is the Joshua Ministry Phase I?

   _____

   _____

   _____

2. Name the two key words in this strategy.

   1. _____
   2. _____

3. What are the fivefold ministry purposes of the church?

   1. _____
   2. _____
   3. _____
   4. _____
   5. _____

Chapter III

The Joshua Ministry Phase II: Churches Helping Churches— The Unity of the Faith

The Joshua Ministry Phase II is bringing all of our efforts together to evangelize to all persons. The command of Jesus was to go to Jerusalem, Judea, and Samaria (Acts 1:8), and to the highways and hedges (Luke 14:23) to share the Gospel. I praise God for any method of evangelism that wins any lost person. However, if we only concern ourselves with those we know personally, then our witness is only a Jerusalem witness. I once attended a seminar where the facilitator stated that after witnessing to his friends and relatives, he had run out of persons with whom to share Christ. As I sat there, I thought about the subdivision next to the church and the set of apartments down the street. Was this congregation only concerned with their families, co-workers, and friends? What about those who lived across the street or down the street? Whose responsibility was it to share God's plan of salvation to them? Would they die in their sin and never be introduced to the Savior of the world? How much longer would they have lived in a hopeless state of gloom and despair? It's interesting to me to hear ministries that started with such fire, using every method and talking to everyone they could, now say that God is leading them only to witness to persons they know. While I don't doubt God told them to witness, it would be inconsistent with God's character or Word to say He told them to only witness to friends and loved ones. Every pastor that has planted a church used the door-to-door method to start his church. I do understand that there are those who have a problem with knocking on doors. It is true, however, based on statistics, that personal evangelism is the most effective way to evangelize. My concern is (1) Are we using personal evangelism to cover up our fear to leave our comfort zone? and (2) Is our Gospel a Gospel that segregates us from other ethnic groups? If this fits you or your congregation, then you're in disobedience to God.

Jonah was disobedient to God when he thought he could do something else. God said go to Nineveh, but Jonah thought he could go to Tarshish. Jonah didn't want to minister to the people of Nineveh. Going to Nineveh meant leaving his comfort zone and his people. However, by using the strategy "Members Helping Members" in our neighborhoods, we don't have to confine our evangelism efforts to our family and friends. To be successful using this method, one must meet needs and have a good follow-up strategy. Yes, you can go into a cold market (where you don't know anyone), develop relationships and have results. What about those we don't know who are dying all around us? Their blood will be required at someone's hands. In order to obey Acts 1:8, to go into Jerusalem, Judea, and Samaria, we have to reach out beyond those we personally know. We are called to go beyond our Jerusalem (our comfort zone). Going beyond our comfort zone, to those we don't personally know, is what I call "inducing labor." As I stated above, in such cases, building relationships, placing our efforts in the community, and getting involved in the lives of our neighbors is imperative if we are to avoid the chance of a spiritual miscarriage or a stillborn birth. If we only minister to those in our own financial, racial, or social circles, then we segregate the Gospel of Christ. If our evangelism doesn't include all people, then it's not what Jesus died for or intends for it to be. What kind of witness does this demonstrate to the world? The strategy "Members Helping Members" brings a workable solution to this need.

Unity

The tribes in Joshua chapter one were to *help* their brothers take possession of the land, a joint effort—unity. These were brothers helping brothers. Hopefully, the brothers did not decide to help their brothers because of the promise of the land they would receive once their mission was completed. It would be nice to think that their help wasn't based on what they would gain, but what they were willing to give, and their brothers would receive. However, based on what we see today in the body of Christ, there are some of us who are only concerned with our own so-called ministry. This is a selfish spirit and will only keep the body of Christ fragmented. Pastor James Brown of Decatur, Georgia, made the following statement to me: "If your vision doesn't include other people, your vision isn't from God." The world will not be won by one church or one organization, but by the body of Christ functioning as one unit. Throughout the history of our country, there have been major events that have caused us to unify, such as war, strikes, and the Civil Rights Movement. How much more would God's kingdom benefit if we would help each other? By putting together our resources, we could accomplish so much more. God used persecution in the Book of Acts to spread the Gospel beyond Jerusalem. I sincerely hope He doesn't have to use persecution again, this time, to bring us together as one unit.

The unity of the faith is what I believe is the common ground between all Protestant churches or what makes us one. I believe this common ground is the blood of Jesus and salvation that comes only through Him. If a person believes that salvation is through Jesus Christ and His blood has been applied to his or her life, then through the redemption process, we are in the same family. It's through the sacrificial life of Jesus that we have received forgiveness for all of our sins; that's what makes us one. While we may have some doctrinal points that are different, at least we have this one biblical truth in common. This biblical truth should be the common ground to bring unity to a fragmented body. It's amazing that in our country, while we let issues such as race divide us, most catastrophes unite us. For example, when war breaks out we all seem to unify against one common enemy. Don't all Christians have the same common enemy? Jesus prayed that those who believed through the disciples would be *one*, "that the world would know Him."

What kind of impact do you think there would be, if we could come together against the only real common enemy we have, the devil, and take salvation to a world that longs to see the manifestation of the sons of God? What kind of impact would it make in our communities to see *not* a Jehovah's Witness at the door, but Christians from different churches and denominations sharing the message that Jesus is the only way? The most common comment I hear from unsaved persons is concerning the hypocrisy of the church, and the different views we have from church to church. One of my son's teachers became a Jehovah's Witness because she was confused by the different beliefs she found from one church to the other. The devil has used confusion, division, deception, and selfishness far too long in order to keep the Body from coming together, *"that the world may believe on Him."* Through prayer and the joint efforts of all, we can see God's hand move in a mighty way; we would witness the greatest harvest of souls the world has ever seen. If we were to lay aside our doctrinal differences and agree that salvation is only through Jesus, we would bring unity to a fragmented body and demonstrate to the world a real Christ.

Another step to bring unity to the body of Christ would be to bring our gifts, talents, and resources together. If we could do this, we could do great things for God. Isn't that what it's all about—His purpose and His glory? Deception that keeps the body of Christ from coming together is very critical as it relates to a lost soul. Just think of the blood that's on our hands every time someone is lost because we haven't done our job; thereby, allowing division to hinder salvation of the lost. When we let ethnic, financial, social, and doctrinal differences separate us, we demonstrate to the world a fragmented Body. If the Body is broken and in need of healing itself, how then can it heal the needs of others?

God never makes things difficult; we do. The strategy is simple. However, the difficult task is to bring us together in unity, and then to commit to the work. The world is not going to be saved by one church or one denomination, but by the body of believers working together as one unit. We must not allow these barriers to keep us from the great harvest of souls that awaits us. Have we not read of the joy and rejoicing in heaven over one soul that receives Christ? Do we not desire the rewards that are laid up for those who labor in the fields to win the lost? Can we not see that, in the light of a life coming to Jesus Christ, the views and doctrinal differences separating us are meaningless? This might sound redundant, but I must say it again and hope you hear it by the Spirit. God wants the Gospel to reach beyond the walls of our churches (beyond Jerusalem). God used persecution to spread the Gospel in the early days of the church. I hope He doesn't have to resort to something similar to get our attention. What would be the eternal effects if we could accomplish this task? We must begin to appreciate the diversity of gifts, talents, culture, and ethnicity within the body of Christ in order for the Body to function as a complete unit. My prayer is that God would open our eyes to the deception that keeps the Body fragmented.

It's interesting that the same confusion that existed at the Tower of Babel in Genesis 11 still exists today. Confusion is not only in the world, but also in the body of Christ. Before they became confused at the Tower of Babel, they were unified. God confused their language so they couldn't accomplish their task. If God hadn't confused their language, only God knows what they could have accomplished. Their task was evil, but they may have accomplished it because they were unified. What if the body of Christ could unify as they did? Jesus prayed in John 17 that He be glorified, the disciples sanctified, and those that believed on their words unified. The unity of the Body has not come to pass yet. However, I believe Jesus' prayer will be answered. The same spirit that caused division at the Tower of Babel is the same spirit that now births us into His body when we cry, "Abba, Father." Those who believe all the signs of His coming have been fulfilled are missing this truth. The prayer of Jesus hasn't been fulfilled yet; therefore, he can't come until we unify. Unity within the Body creates a resource pool of gifts, talents and resources that help fulfill the visions of those who lack the resources, causing the world to see a visible Christ through His body—the church. Again, Jesus said that when we come together in unity, it would cause the world to believe in Him (John 17:15-21).

One-Year Strategy

I believe that each city, regardless of size, could be evangelized in one year. If each church, having the common ground of salvation through Christ, would come together, divide the target neighborhoods into blocks, going street by street, door by door, block by block, sharing Christ and meeting needs until the next assigned area is reached, each city could be taken. However, this strategy can only be accomplished when all churches and denominations that confess salvation in Jesus Christ come together as one unit. Each church would be responsible for a twelve-block area in which to share Christ and meet needs.

Another strategy is to have churches in the same zip code, because of the common interest they have in the community, come together going door by door sharing Christ and meeting needs. We are only sharing Christ and not doctrinal views. Whenever members talked with people they could give the person a list of churches in the participating community. This would allow the prospect the freedom to choose a new church home. The churches could also go out representing only one church in the area using that church's material. The same effort would then be duplicated in the community of participating churches. There are too many lost persons in each community to fight over where they belong. Being possessive over an area only demonstrates a territorial spirit and not the Spirit of Christ. In order for this strategy to work, each church must help in the fields of their brothers the same way farmers used to do years ago. Farmers do help each other today, but I am sure we can agree that there is a real absence of the spirit of community in the world today.

Churches in the same zip code that share the same interest in the community as the residents will also share the responsibility for doing follow-up. If a church doesn't agree to share in the work, then they can't share in the harvest. We must also equip our members through the teaching ministry to evangelize in their communities. It's my suggestion that an evangelism workshop be held prior to going out into the community. This would provide teaching for those who have never been out, and help sharpen the skills of those whose skills may be dull. After the seminar, those who are experienced should pair up with those who have little or no experience. This same process will then be duplicated in the communities of those churches that helped in the preceding effort.

Let's remember the great harvest that the disciples gathered in Luke 5. The disciples had fished all night and had not caught anything. Nevertheless, at the command of Jesus they let down their nets and caught so many fish that others had to help them gather in the catch. The great harvest they received would have never been gathered without the help of others. How much could we get done if churches could come together and help each other bring in the harvest? The one-year strategy is simple. It doesn't have to take years to possess our land; we can do it in one year if we work together.

Existing Ministries

The utilization of existing ministries is the key to moving a ministry with no resources to becoming a resource center. In 1 Corinthians 12, Paul uses an analogy of the church of Christ as a human body. This analogy speaks of the unity of the Body when respective parts are in their place doing what they were designed to do. If we would accept that each member has a gift or talent to contribute, but are of the same body, then we could accomplish great things for God's kingdom. If we were to allow each part to function in its proper place, without being afraid of another particular part receiving more attention, then the Body would function as it was designed. Each member has a part to contribute in order for the Body to achieve its maximum performance. Likewise, each church has a gift or talent to contribute. Each person that receives salvation through Jesus Christ is part of His body. We seem to want our own things, such as buildings and resources, without helping others. The question is, however, How productive are we? We will spend years without the resources to do effective ministry, when our needs could be met through an existing ministry. The Bible says, "Hope deferred makes the heart sick" (Prov. 13:12, NIV). If we lack resources and allow pride or anything else to stop us from working together, our unfulfilled dream will make our hearts sick. For example, if you are waiting to start an outreach ministry without support ministries in place, your vision is put on hold, you become discouraged while you spend years raising money to build and supply for that outreach ministry. Then, if you do get things in place, you are too old and have no strength to complete the vision. There are those who die unfulfilled because they were unable to complete the vision God had placed in their hearts.

Using existing ministries means using others' gifts, talents, and resources. If your church does not have a social ministry to provide such things as clothing and food, then by using an existing ministry, such as the Salvation Army, your ministry could continue while you're still building. The key is Jesus Christ and salvation through His redemptive work. Doesn't this qualify ministries like the Salvation Army as well as others as part of the Body? At this point, we're just talking about churches working together and not other agencies (even though other agencies can also be used to assist in meeting the needs of others). The most important thing is to be a channel to meet the needs of those who seek help, so you will have an opportunity to share Christ with them. If we could do this, think of the goals, dreams, and visions that would be fulfilled. Think of the unproductive years that could be turned into productive years for God. Have we ever thought about how many people die without Christ while we're trying to get everything in place? Think of the unity this would bring to the Body and the glory it would bring to God. This would also release more gifts in the Body. What effect would it have on a world that waits to see the manifestation of the sons of God?

There are great benefits for using existing ministries:

1. Helps fulfill your call
2. Creates unity within the Body
3. Demonstrates unity to the world, that they may know Him
4. Brings resources together
5. Allows the Christian to work within his or her gifted area of ministry

Chapter III Questions

Joshua Ministry Phase II — Churches Helping Churches

1. What would unifying the Body demonstrate to the world? _____
   _____

2. List five components that will put the one-year strategy into action.

   1. _____
   2. _____
   3. _____
   4. _____
   5. _____

3. What are the benefits of utilizing existing ministries?

   1. _____
   2. _____
   3. _____
   4. _____
   5. _____

CHAPTER IV
The Joshua Ministry Phase III
The Joshua Generation: God's Witnessing Army

In Joshua 4:6, the children of Israel were to communicate to their children how God had brought them across the Jordan River. In the same manner, we must accept the responsibility of sharing how God's great power of deliverance took us out of the bondage of sin. By sharing our experience with others, the door will then be opened for us to share how God can change their lives. It would also teach them how they can communicate the Gospel to their peers—one generation to the next communicating what God has done.

The Joshua Generation: God's Witnessing Army are the teenagers, those the world has labeled Generation X, but who we believe are going to be greatly used by God. They're not worthless as some would say, but they are of great value in God's army. This group has the potential to be a witnessing army with the same spirit and courage that Joshua exhibited.

It was during a teen conference at Greenforest Community Baptist Church in 1999 that the tract entitled "Teen Evangelism" was added. During this effort, fifteen souls received Jesus Christ for the first time. Teens get very excited when God uses them to make a difference in another teenager's life. I find that teens are very relational and are concerned about the problems of other teens. Excitement and concern are two areas that motivate teens to minister to others.

It almost seems to be an impossible task to win our own children and other teens to Christ. However, I would like to share what we did in our own home when one of our children came under attack by the enemy, and then share a complete evangelism program for teens. At the age of fifteen, our middle son D'Juan, didn't want anything to do with God or the church. I don't need to go into a lot of details concerning what happened; however, those who have had a teen rebel against God understand what it is like for the parents going through such a phase/ordeal. This is what God led us to do and how He brought victory into our home within a few months.

In God's Word I found principles that I could use to bring tremendous change within my own family. The principles are found in Mark 5:22 and Mark 7:25. In Mark 5, we have the story of Jairus who came to Jesus because his daughter was sick and later died. In chapter seven, we have the story of the Syrophenician woman who wanted Jesus to cast an unclean spirit out of her daughter. In both stories there were three principles that were used, and as a result the parent received the child back.

The first thing is they had faith; even when the condition became worse they still believed God. Sometimes when we pray and we see things get worse, we take it out of God's hand; however, we must *stay in faith*. The second thing that each of them did was to fall down and worship Jesus. Notice, they didn't complain or get an attitude towards God or ask why, they simply praised Him. God's Word admonishes us to *give God praise in all things*, not for the situation, but in the midst of the situation. The third thing the parents did was they besought Him, they asked Him, and made a request unto Him to get involved. What is God saying? What does God want to do? How does He want to do it? When we have problems we tend to tell God what to do and how to do it, when instead we should *find out His will and purpose* for the situation.

In 1 Kings 17:17-22, there is another principle. Here we find Elijah who took a dead boy and laid him across his bed, cried unto the Lord, and stretched himself upon the child three times. As he cried to God, the child's spirit returned unto him again. This principle teaches us that sometimes we need to get down, lay prostrate before the Lord, and as I say, "just get a hold of the altar" until God moves. We must have patience. God will move in our teens' lives if we use these principles found in His Word. They worked in my family.

Teens want to belong to and identify with something. For whatever reason, the lack of family interaction in the home has caused our teens to look elsewhere for a real sense of belonging. Hence, the gang in too many cases fits the bill. This generation is the first generation in history predicated to do worse than their parents did. Our society has already concluded that they are not going to amount to anything, and has marked them. We have marked them X, a generation with no hope. However, The Joshua Generation: God's Witnessing Army concept gives teens a sense of identity and purpose that they are searching for. I believe God has great things in store for this group. As I talk to teens, I have found that they are very hungry. The hunger is for something real. However, as they look at the church at large, they say they haven't seen anything that's real. Teens say church people are hypocritical because they say one thing and do another. If the church could show them a real Christ, they would be drawn to Him.

The singing and shouting we do does not demonstrate to them a living Christ when we live a different lifestyle at home. In most cases, teens can sing and shout circles around us. To reach them, we're not talking about changing God's Word, but using the principles of God's unchanging Word. It does not change. It worked yesterday and it works today. The hunger our youth have can be a starting point to meet our youth where they are. Then we can introduce them to Christ and give them a true sense of belonging.

Once a teen has given his or her life to Christ, that youth will have a real sense of concern for his other peers. Teens want their friends to receive the same living Christ they have received. I don't know if we noticed it or not, but in the wake of the school shootings, the first place kids turned to was the church! They do believe in spiritual things and want to be connected to spiritual things. We must show them the way to a true and living Christ. I believe God is going to use this so-called "Generation X" in a great way. The church seems to be like Israel when they came to the Promised Land the first time. They were full of fear and would not cross over to possess the land God had already given to them. While most of us are full of fear and remain chained to our pews, this is a fearless generation that knows no limits and loves to take risks. God can use these characteristics in a great way. I have found that once teens form a relationship with Christ, they are on fire and want to win the world. I have seen them go into their schools with boldness and witness to their friends. They're not afraid to tell their friends about the love of Christ or to confront the sin in their friend's lives. They don't care where they share Christ. I believe that as adults, if we don't move out of our comfort zones, God is going to raise them up to do what we refuse to do. Like Joshua, they don't fear and don't mind stepping out, while most of us struggle in these areas. In Joshua 5:7, we are told that God raised up their children in their stead. If they can belong to Satan's gang, why not God's army? Let's not X them out like the world, but pray that God may use them to move out towards others.

Teen Evangelism Program

Our youth are confronted with a world of problems, including drugs, teen pregnancy, suicide, confusion, gangs, violence, dysfunctional families, and other stressful things. However, there are several common denominators that I have noticed within all teens that when properly understood and directed, become common factors and points of ministry or can serve as the release of ministry.

Most teens seem to struggle with acceptance, identity, and purpose. While at the same time, they are concerned for the misfortune of others and the condition of the world. I believe one of the causes of the rebellion among our teens is that they're reaching out for love and acceptance. However, gangs are not a real place of love and acceptance. The love and acceptance that gangs offer is distorted. It leaves no real solution for a world full of real problems.

My own teenage children, and hundreds of others at the high school and college level, are consistently involved in community projects. One of the ministries at Greenforest is a ministry that feeds the homeless every Saturday. I have noticed a large youth presence in this ministry. These teens do not have to be here, but they willingly volunteer their service. I have also noticed that every week the Feed the Homeless Ministry meets, it's not always the same group of teens volunteering. Why? Because they are concerned about certain conditions in our society. This concern for the less fortunate and world affairs is a good place to get them involved in ministry. Their concern for world events and the plight of others who are less fortunate identify points of passion and ministry within their group. When teens are released to work in these areas, it will bring fulfillment and direct them to purpose for their lives. We can ascertain from these events that they look for purpose, acceptance, and fulfillment. Purpose and fulfillment can only be found in a relationship with Jesus Christ. Once we enter into a real relationship with Him, we will then understand that we are accepted in the beloved (Eph. 1:6).

With purpose and fulfillment as a base, the following Gospel presentation was developed for teens. When I witness to teens, starting my presentation with an opening statement, "God has a purpose for your life," without exception, the teens look at me with a puzzled or questioning look on their faces. This indicates that they are looking for purpose, thus opening the door to talk to them about the void God has put within the hearts of all men. Purpose and the void are what they are really seeking to discover.

The following is an outline of the Gospel presentation:

Introduction

Teens have their own dialogue. With that in mind, it's my suggestion to allow them to engage in their own normal conversation. From this point, the following diagnostic question can be asked so one can begin to talk to them about spiritual matters.

Diagnostic Question

List some of the things you and your friends do together, such as activities, places visited, and even bad things or habits done together (i.e., movies, smoking). Then ask them this question: Do you still feel like something is missing, or do you still feel unfulfilled? If they answer yes, say:

Witness: I feel the same way. Can I share with you what I have discovered? Wait for a response.

Witness: That unfulfilled feeling we have inside is a void that God has put in all of us. Now, I don't know how you feel about God or church, but let me share with you what I found out. When God created us, He placed within all of us a void that leads us down a road trying to find acceptance, purpose, and fulfillment for our lives. We're trying to fill a void that can only be satisfied when we accept Jesus and His plan for our life.

Transition

Do you ever think about spiritual things? Did you know God has a purpose for your life? Or say, Do you want that hunger on the inside to be satisfied?

I. God wants us to have
    a. A successful life now (John 10:10).
    b. Eternal life (John 3:16).

Eternal life is a free gift (Rom. 6:23). Have you received God's free gift of eternal life?

Transition

The reason the void is in our life is because of sin.

II. A universal problem
- a. All have sinned (Rom. 3:23)
- b. God has to judge sin (Rom. 6:23a)

Transition

The only way we can solve the sin problem, fill the void, and find real purpose in life is to come into a relationship with Jesus Christ. The way we do this is to:

III. Repent
- a. "Repent ye therefore, and be converted, that your sins may be blotted out" (Acts 3:19). Repent means to live a different lifestyle than we do now.
- b. Sin has to be judged. The payment for sin is death, but God's free gift to us is eternal life through Jesus Christ (Rom. 6:23).

IV. Accept and place our faith in what God has done through Jesus
- a. God became flesh in the person of Jesus Christ (John 1:14)
- b. God placed our sin on Him (Is. 53:6; 1 Pet. 3:18)
- c. By grace are we saved by faith (Eph. 2:8)

      d. For those who accept Him, He gives the right to become His son (John 1:12)

V. Surrender our life to Jesus
      a. Confess with our mouth and believe in our heart (Rom. 10:9-10)
      b. He saves us even though we don't deserve to be saved, by only trusting in Him. Salvation is a free gift from Him (Eph. 2:8)
      c. Confess publicly/pray openly (Matt. 10:23, 33)

VI. Prayer of commitment

"Dear heavenly Father, I am a sinner, but I've heard the good news today that Jesus died for my sins. I ask you to forgive me for all of my sins. I believe in my heart, and confess with my mouth that Jesus died on the cross for my sins and was raised from the dead, and right now I accept Him and receive Him as my Lord and Savior."

There are four things that sinners need to include while praying this prayer. First, there must be an acknowledgement of their sin(s). Second, they must ask for forgiveness of their sin. Third, they must believe that Jesus died for their sin. And, fourth, they must accept Jesus into their life by faith according to Romans 10:9-10.

The Scriptures above can be spoken in a manner that teens can better understand, perhaps if spoken in their own vernacular. We have to remember that this is not the sixteenth century, and the King James English is not the language we use today. The following Scriptures can be used to bring assurance to those who accept Christ.

VII. Assurance of salvation Scriptures

    a. He that believes on Christ has eternal life (John 6:47)

    b. I give unto them eternal life (John 10:28)

Personal Testimony

Another way teens can share the Gospel is by sharing their testimony. The personal testimony is one of the strongest tools we have. People can dispute the Bible all day long, but one's personal experience is factual. In Acts 26, Paul gives his personal testimony before King Agrippa. His testimony consisted of three parts: his life before Christ, his salvation experience, and his life since receiving Christ. On the following page write your personal testimony. Bo Mitchell, a teacher and great soul winner in the body of Christ, suggests starting your testimony by asking, "May I share with you the most exciting thing that has ever happened to me?" And, he suggests ending your testimony by asking, "Has anything like this ever happened to you?"

Before Christ _____

_____
_____

Salvation Experience _____
_____
_____
_____
_____
_____
_____
_____

Since Christ _____
_____
_____
_____
_____
_____
_____
_____
_____

Let's not miss the opportunity to share our own personal testimony with our children, and then teach them to share their story with others, especially their peers.

Chapter IV Questions

The Joshua Ministry Phase III — The Joshua Generation: God's Witnessing Army

1. What are the Scriptures and principles found to help us win our teens?

    1. _____
    2. _____
    3. _____

2. Name the two interests teens have that can be used for ministry.

    1. _____
    2. _____

3. Name the four ingredients of the sinner's prayer.

    1. _____
    2. _____
    3. _____
    4. _____

CHAPTER V
Joshua Ministry Phase IV: Special Forces

Just as Joshua had a special group to go before their brothers (Joshua 1:14-15), this unit, called "Special Forces," helps pastors in the area of planting new churches. The Special Forces unit is also trained to evangelize at night. Night evangelism, is about reaching persons in our society who do most of their activity at night. This special unit is trained to reach these lost persons who are filled with hopelessness and despair, many of whom do not love their own lives.

A great number of these persons are held in bondage to a lifestyle from which they desire to be free. Satan has great influence in their lives. One of the greatest problems in ministering to these persons is getting past the shame they feel because of sin. They feel they can't come to God because of their sin. We must become intercessors for them and help them get free from a life filled with hopelessness and despair. We can't assume that they can break free on their own—they need help. Satan has some of them held captive against their will. Therefore, we cannot write them off under the assumption that God has given us the right to decide who is or is not worthy to make it into His kingdom.

If you think about it, most of us look down on this group of people. However, this is one of the groups Jesus would be found ministering to if He were physically on earth today. These people are hurting and are in bondage to a hard taskmaster—Satan. The "Special Forces" unit reaches out to these hurt and lost people.

Two of Satan's biggest tools are fear and deception. He uses these two tools to immobilize us. Many don't believe me when I tell them that I have the same apprehension they do when going into the field. We must understand that it's Satan's job to use these two tools to keep us immobile. If we are to be successful, we must move out in faith beyond fear and deception. When we move out, there must always be an element of faith. In my experience, when we do step out to witness to a family member, a co-worker, door-to-door, at night, or in a less desirable area, God will meet us there. God will give you boldness (Acts 4:31) and words to say (Luke 12:12).

All of us are either filled with God's Spirit, or we are filled with fear—the devil's spirit. One experiences tremendous joy and fulfillment when sharing Christ with a lost person, or seeing a life changed from the kingdom of darkness to the kingdom of light. This joy and fulfillment can only take place as we allow God to use us. We will then wonder why it took so long for us to allow God to use us in such an awesome way. I have heard people make statements like, "I wish I had done this years ago." You will find that you will make the same statement when you step out and witness for the first time. We will never experience this manifestation until we first move out in faith. It's in the darkest places that God's power will be manifested the most.

The safest place is in God's will. A person once said he would rather be walking through a minefield in the total will of God than to be in the comfort of his home out of God's will. God needs us to be His hands, mouth, and feet. As we walk in His will, He will protect us. However, if something were to happen to us, it would be better if it were to happen while we are in His will, than if we were out of His will. Believe me when I say God has to help all of us in this area. However, perfect love casts out fear because fear will only keep us in torment (1 John 4:18). If we live in fear, we haven't been made perfect in love towards God. This love can only come as we spend time in prayer and God's Word. Fear and deception can only be overcome through prayer and a working knowledge of God's Word. This is the only way we can reach men and women from all walks of life.

God has led the Special Forces unit on what many might consider some strange assignments. We went to a liquor store and began to share the Gospel with those going in and out of the store. After about fifteen minutes, the owner of the store asked the police to have us leave. God was making an impact on the people going in and out of the store. As we witnessed, the Holy Spirit convicted the hearts of those with whom we shared. We were only there fifteen minutes before the police asked us to leave! The police officer did not have a problem with what we were doing; but apologizing, he did his job. As we boarded the church van one of the members on the team was praying with someone to receive Christ. It was an exciting experience.

On the Fourth of July, the Lord led the team to an abortion clinic in downtown Atlanta. The clinic was closed. We were to march around the clinic like the children of Israel did at Jericho. As we ended our assignment, I looked up to see a man directly in front of me. As I went to the man and engaged in conversation with him, he began to say, "I saw you." I ask him did he mean that he saw us walking around the building? His answer was no. He said that God had shown him my face the night before, and he knew we would be down at the clinic that day. The man prayed to receive Christ. The gentleman was a businessman who had a business next door to the clinic. Note his faith: he went to the clinic when it was closed. His business was also closed. It was a holiday; all of us could have been doing something else. However, the Spirit of God said go. If we had not gone, we would have missed our divine appointment and been in disobedience to God. God manifested Himself and gave us a testimony.

God has even led us to go to a nightclub where two received Christ. I am sure there are those who have a problem with us going to these kinds of establishments. However, if Jesus were physically here today, He would be in the same places doing the same things.

Chapter V Questions

Joshua Ministry Phase IV: Special Forces

1. What are two of Satan's biggest tools?

   1. _____
   2. _____

2. What two weapons do we have to use against Satan's tools?

   1. _____
   2. _____

Chapter VI
Possessing the Promised Land

Possessing the Promised Land was a joint effort between God, leadership, and the people. Victory was assured as long as all three parts worked together as ONE UNIT. God would certainly do His part, but what about leadership (Joshua) and the people he was leading? What would guarantee their success? Within the Book of Joshua, we looked at a strategy and principles that will guarantee the success of both the leader and the people while accomplishing possession of the Promised Land. The following Scriptures show us that we all have a part to play in the possession of the land. Anything less than a joint effort will result in possible failure. God has a role. The church leadership has a role. And, the members of the congregation have a role.

God's Role

God's role is evident in the promises in Joshua 1:2-5:

1. Give them the land
2. Do not let any man stand before them
3. Be with them

4. Will not fail them nor forsake them

5. Prosper them

God has given us the same promises. However, we sit in our pews expecting God to do all the work. He has already done the work, but we will never see Him fulfill His part until we first move out. Every promise that we believe for God to fulfill and every assignment that God gives us always requires an element of faith. God's assignment for us will always be too big for us to handle; thus causing us to depend on Him, so He will receive all the glory. There are even those who say they need to pray about witnessing. They are wasting their time praying about something that God has already commanded us to do. We all have been given a ministry to reconcile men back to God (2 Cor. 5:17-19). God's power is not released until one begins to move out in faith. Sometimes, when God gives a promise, we have to walk it out by faith or go through circumstances before what we are believing God for will actually manifest itself. It seems that many of us expect the lost to just come to God by themselves without any effort from the saints. There is a principle of seedtime and harvest (Mark 4); however, we have to plant a seed first before we receive a harvest. God will fulfill all of His promises to us—we can count on that.

Leadership Role

Principles for Joshua's successful leadership are found in Deuteronomy 31:3, 7, 14-15, and Joshua 1:1-9. In

Deuteronomy 31:3, God tells Moses to tell the people that Joshua would lead them over Jordan. In verse 14, Moses is told to bring Joshua to the tabernacle of the congregation, "that I may give him a charge." In verse 15, a pillar of cloud came down, representing God's presence upon His servant, Joshua. Moses then presented Joshua before the people. However, Joshua did not assume the position of leadership at that time, but he remained faithful under the leadership of Moses until God's fullness of time. The time for him to lead the people didn't come until much later. Joshua became the leader after Moses' death. We can learn from Joshua's example that we cannot lead until we first follow. God will never give us what belongs to us until we are first faithful to another's leadership (Luke 16:10-16).

These verses in Deuteronomy and Joshua 1:1-2 show us that Joshua's success was according to principles he practiced:

1. He was called by God and confirmed before men.
2. He was both faithful and submissive to authority.
3. He was anointed for ministry, functioning in his area of calling.
4. He was patient—he did not go ahead of God, but waited on God's time.
5. He moved out in faith.
6. He was willing to leave his comfort zone.

7. He was mindful of God's promise.

8. He was obedient to God's Word.

9. He was strong and courageous.

10. He was able to speak and explain God's Word.

11. He maintained a devotional life.

12. He followed God's direction.

Joshua's success rested on him remembering God's promises and obeying His Word. In verses three through five, God's promise was that every place Joshua and the children of Israel placed their feet would be theirs. God promised to be with Joshua as he had been with Moses. Joshua was also told to be strong and courageous. To be strong meant to be fortified or to be obstinate. To be courageous meant to be steadfast minded, strong, established, and hardened. Joshua was also told in verse nine not to be afraid and dismayed. This meant not to be beat down or discouraged, scared, or terrified. He was told to keep the law with the promise that he would prosper or to push forward, or to break out and be profitable. By keeping God's law, he would prosper and have good success, or be able to deal wisely in all the affairs of life. Joshua's success as leader depended on him remembering God's promise, being strong and courageous, observing to do all the Law, not turning to the right or the left, speaking and meditating on God's Word, applying the Word, being led by God, and not being afraid or dismayed (vv. 2-9).

The People's Role

Even though God had given them the land through His promise, the people still had to do something to possess the land (Joshua 1:10-18; 2:3, 5, 15; 3:5; 4:3; 6:5-6). Their success depended upon them:

1. Not living in the past (leadership had changed).

2. Physically taking the land.

3. Leaving from where they were.

4. Submitting to authority.

5. Making preparation.

6. Remembering the promises of God.

7. Helping their brothers until victory was assured.

8. Sanctifying themselves and not serving strange gods.

9. Leaving a sign for future generations.

10. Entering into a covenant with God.

11. Following the presence of God.

12. Remembering lessons from the past (wilderness).

Lessons From the Wilderness

There are other lessons that we can learn from the children of Israel. If we do not learn these lessons, we will find ourselves wandering around in circles, just as they did. If we continue to go around in circles, the land will never be possessed. The generation that came to the banks of the Jordan was not the same generation that had been there forty years before. Their parents had died in the wilderness over a period of forty years. This generation could have made the same mistakes their forefathers made. In Deuteronomy 1:26-32, there are five reasons given why they didn't enter the Promised Land:

1. The people rebelled
2. They murmured
3. They allowed the report of their brothers to discourage them
4. Their eyes deceived them
5. They just did not believe God

According to Deuteronomy 8, the wilderness was a place to humble them and prove what was in their heart and whether or not they would serve God. When Israel left Egypt, God took them through different experiences that would prepare them for their wilderness journey, and eventually their entrance and possession of the Promised Land. God does the same to us through our experiences. When they came out of Egypt, God led them to a place called The Wilderness of the Red Sea. God purposefully led them there and allowed them to be hedged in. When Pharaoh saw they were hedged in, he pursued after them; but God fought for them. From this experience, they should have learned that God would fight their battles (Ex. 13:17—14:31).

In Exodus 15:22-26, God proved them by taking them to the Wilderness of Shur. After going three days into the wilderness, they found no water, and they came to a place called Marah. The water they found here was bitter, and they couldn't drink it. Moses put a branch in the water, and the water became sweet. It was here at Marah that they should have learned that God would provide healing for His people. After this, God led them to a place called Elim—a place where there was water and rest. It's in the midst of our experiences that God will also give us refreshing, and prepare for us a table in the presence of our enemies.

In chapter 16, God led them to the Wilderness of Sin. It was here the people complained and wanted food. Here again, God was preparing them: He provided bread from heaven and meat to eat. The lesson they should have learned from this was that God was their provider. From these wilderness lessons they were to learn that:

1. God would fight their battles.
2. God was their healer.
3. God would provide for them.

In Deuteronomy 1 they were to leave the mountain of God and go to Kadesh-Barnea, an eleven-day journey. The number eleven is the number that means imperfection. Had they gone one more day, they would have journeyed twelve days. The number twelve means governmental authority or the authority of God. They remained in imperfection by only going eleven days. In chapter two, after doubting God's ability to fight for them, God told Moses to take them back to the Wilderness of the Red Sea. This is where they should have learned earlier that God would fight for them, but they hadn't learned their lesson. (Do we sometimes wonder why we keep going around in the same circle? Maybe we haven't learned our lesson yet.) This didn't seem to be a problem with the new generation, this time they crossed over Jordan. They allowed God to fight for them. However, if they had not learned these lessons at some point, it could have also prevented their successful entrance into the Promised Land. If we don't learn what God is teaching us through our experiences, we will never be able to cross over our Jordan and possess the Promised Land that's set before us.

As we continue to experience the same problems, these are lessons we need to learn. These lessons are to prepare us to possess the land. Unlearned lessons will only hinder our success and the harvest of lost souls from being gathered. In other words, if we continue to let the same hindrances (fear, doubt, anxiety, lack of resources, or whatever) keep us from obeying God, we will continue to go around in circles struggling with the same problems. This will only cause frustration, disappointment, lack of fulfillment, and a harvest that will die in the field.

Once fruit is ripened, if it is not picked it will go bad. One of the ways you know sinners (fruit) are ripe for harvest is by their addiction to filling the hunger inside. However, if the fruit is not harvested in time, they will begin to get involved in things neither you nor they thought they would. Initially, they may start out small, but before long they are way out there in sin. This is a good indication that the fruit is beyond the point of picking. At this point, it will take some real effort to salvage it. A soul that is not harvested will die on the vine. He will drift further and further away from God. Nothing is impossible with God, He can bring them in. However, there would have been less effort on our part to harvest them. This would have also kept them from gravitating further into a life of sin. We need to discern when the fruit is ready for harvest, and then pick it.

Chapter VI Questions

The Joshua Ministry: Possessing the Promised Land

1. What was God's role in possessing the land?

    1. _____
    2. _____
    3. _____
    4. _____
    5. _____

2. What were the principles that made Joshua's leadership successful?

    1. _____
    2. _____
    3. _____
    4. _____
    5. _____
    6. _____
    7. _____
    8. _____

9. _____
10. _____
11. _____
12. _____

3. What things did the people have to do for success?

    1. _____
    2. _____
    3. _____
    4. _____
    5. _____
    6. _____
    7. _____
    8. _____
    9. _____
    10. _____
    11. _____
    12. _____

4. Name five things that hinder us from entering into the Promised Land.

    1. _____
    2. _____

3. _____
4. _____
5. _____

5. What are the three lessons God teaches us through our experiences?

   1. _____
   2. _____
   3. _____

CHAPTER VII

Where Do We Begin?

I believe the answer to this question can be found in prayer, praise, worship, and what I call the four Ts—Teaching, Training, Tally, and Testimony, which will be discussed in the next chapter.

Prayer, Praise, and Worship

Before we ever try to evangelize, we must pray, praise, and worship. We need to pray over the area, pray for the lost, and use praise and worship as a weapon to break down walls of resistance. In Joshua 6, it was the shout of praise that brought the walls of Jericho down. We must first develop our own personal prayer life; then we can effectively pray for the lost. It's out of a consistent fervent prayer life that one becomes committed and can then say, "Not my will, Lord, but thy will be done." Through prayer we will become more sensitive to the lost, and ascertain God's heart of concern for them. It's through prayer that a passion for the hurting and lost will surface in your own life. You can't spend time with God and not feel what He feels or see what He sees and not respond to it. When we don't feel this compassion in our hearts for those that hurt or are lost, it's a clear indication that we don't spend much time in prayer. When we spend little time in prayer, we will do very little for God. However, when we spend a lot of time in prayer, we will do a considerable amount for God. We must desire His will, which can only come through prayer. It was only after fervent prayer that Jesus was able to submit to God's will for Him to die on the cross. It is important for us to have a good prayer life so that we can pray effectively for laborers and for the lost. When we spend time in prayer, we will become more concerned about the lost and more committed to the purpose of God.

I heard a story a few years ago about three bears — a papa bear, a mama bear, and a baby bear. The story reveals how Noah was able to get all of those animals into the Ark. The story goes something like this: There were three bears walking down a path through the forest when the mama bear said to the papa bear, "Baby Bear is hungry." Papa Bear just kept walking. After a while, Mama Bear said again, "Baby Bear is hungry," Papa Bear just grunted. Mama Bear got angry and started to say something when she heard a noise in the distance getting louder and louder. As they journeyed towards the direction of the sound, they came to the edge of the forest. On the other side was a clearing. As she looked she saw something she had never seen before. What was it? What was it for? And why were they headed for it? When she could not take any more she screamed out, "Papa Bear! Just where do you think you're going?" Papa Bear said, "Over there (towards the ark)." "Why?" said the mother bear. Papa Bear said, "I don't know, I just feel led." There is no possible way Noah could have gotten all those different animals on the Ark without God's Spirit drawing them. Just as there is no possible way that we can effectively do evangelism without God's Spirit leading, directing, speaking, convicting, and drawing the lost. Evangelism without prayer can only result in a stubborn will and a hard heart in those whom we try to reach.

In Joshua 3:3, 11 the people didn't move out unless the Ark of the Covenant, symbolizing God's presence, went before them. Likewise, we must have God's presence out ahead of us to be assured of the victory. We should be like David and inquire of the Lord what direction we should go. David's concern was that God go before him. If God was not going before him, he knew he could not prevail in battle (1 Sam. 30:6). Without prayer we will find ourselves engaged in demonic activity that could have been held back through our efforts in prayer.

The Prayer Ministry at Greenforest Community Baptist Church prays specifically in two areas as it relates to evangelism. The first area is to pray for our members who are chained to the pews with fear. The second area is for the lost who don't know Christ. The list below will show you how to pray effectively for members in a church and for the lost.

Prayer for Members of the Church
We pray:

1. That God releases a spirit of evangelism in the church (Acts 1:8). When the Holy Spirit fell on them, He came with a spirit of evangelism to reach beyond Jerusalem.

2. Against the powers of darkness. These are spirits of apathy, unbelief, and rebellion that hold us in our pews (Dan. 10:13, Eph. 6).

3. That God raises up laborers (Matt. 9:37-38). Jesus said, "The fields were white all ready to harvest, but the laborers were few" (John 4:35). We need to pray that God would raise church members to answer the call to share Christ to a dying world. Jesus said that we should pray to the Lord of Harvest that there would only be a small number of Christians winning the lost, in proportion to the number Christians in the world. That's why we need to pray that God will raise up laborers.

4. That their eyes will be open to God's calling and to the power that is available to them (Eph. 1:18-20). This Scripture specifically teaches us what we should pray for our members. We should pray that God opens

their eyes to His calling, His inheritance, and how much power is available to the one who believes. The power available to those that believe is equivalent to that which raised Christ.

II. Prayer for the Lost

When we pray for the lost, we must pray:

1. That our heavenly Father draws the lost (John 6:44). Only God can draw persons to Himself.
2. Against spiritual blindness (Eph. 1:18-20; 2 Cor. 4:3-4). Although Paul was writing to believers, there is a principle that can be used for the lost as well. We can pray that the eyes of the lost be open so that they may know what the hope of God's calling is for them.
3. The Holy Spirit brings conviction on the person (John 16:8). A man will never see his sin, unless the Holy Spirit reveals it to him. The Holy Spirit has to bring conviction of the sin in one's life.
4. For receptive hearts (Luke 8:5,12). A lost person's heart needs to be broken to receive the seed of the Gospel. Mark 4 reveals different types of ground. The reception of the seed is based on the soil. The soil represents the heart. If the heart is hard, the soil is hard.

If the heart is soft, the soil is fertile ground and can receive the seed of God's Word.

5. God gives them repentance to believe (2 Tim. 2:25). It's God's goodness that leads us to repent (Rom. 2:4).

Intercessory prayer means standing in the gap for the lost (Ezek. 2:30). When we make intercession for someone else, we plead on his or her behalf before God. We have to remember that most unbelievers feel dirty, ashamed, and unworthy; therefore, they feel they can't come to God. Now, we know God wants them to come to Him and repent, but Satan has blinded their minds. It's through prayer that we stand in their stead and help bring them into the presence of God. We should pray that God will open their eyes to see Him and not the church. If they look at the church, Satan will be glad to show them the faults that lie within.

Chapter VII Questions

Where We Begin

1. Where do we begin?

   1. _____
   2. _____
   3. _____
   4. _____
   5. _____

2. When praying for our members, what should we pray?

   1. _____
   2. _____
   3. _____
   4. _____
       a. _____
       b. _____

3. How do we effectively pray for the lost?

   1. _____
   2. _____
   3. _____
   4. _____
   5. _____

Chapter VIII
Four Ts

Along with prayer, there are what I call the four Ts: Teaching, Training, Tally, and Testimony. Like prayer, they educate the student, give life application, accountability, and release fire in the congregation.

Teaching

God's Word comes to break every chain in our lives. The delivering power that accompanies the preached Word will never be seen in the area of evangelism if the message of evangelism is not preached from our pulpits. Today, most messages from our pulpits concern subject matter other than evangelism. God always confirms His Word with signs following (Mark 16:20). We have noticed, when faith is preached, faith manifests itself in the congregation. When salvation is preached, a spiritual birth takes place in the congregation. When prosperity is preached, prosperity comes. When we preach an evangelism message, the spirit of evangelism will manifest in our congregations also.

Along with preaching evangelism, we must also provide teaching from God's Word on the subject of evangelism and the responsibility to witness, which is given to all believers. Evangelism must be taught to all, so that all can share the message of the Gospel. When statements are made like, "Everyone is not called to evangelize," it only indicates a lack of teaching and understanding of God's universal call to the entire Body to win the lost.

While I understand the statement "All are not called," this can only be applied to the *office* of the evangelist, to which all are not called. However, the responsibility to share the Gospel is given to all believers. Teaching and preaching evangelism based on God's Word will equip and help break the fear and apathy that has our congregations chained to the pews. Along with teaching the Great Commission (Matt. 28:19-20), we should teach about the ministry of reconciliation (2 Cor. 5:17-19). This ministry has been given to all believers. We should also teach the three commands of Jesus found in the Book of Matthew:

1. *Come* unto Me (11:28)

2. *Follow* Me (4:19)

3. *Go* into the entire world (28:19)

When we come to Him, we receive salvation. Most of us have done this—we have come to Jesus and received salvation, but some of us have not followed. Jesus said if we would follow Him, He would make us a fisher of people, not pew sitters. If we're not actively fishing for men, it's because we haven't followed Him. The real question is are we truly following the true purpose of Jesus?

We must first understand whose responsibility it is to share the Gospel. There are several Scriptures that command us to go and win the lost, which is the Great Commission. The most familiar Scripture references are Matthew 28:16-20; Mark 16:15-16; Luke 24:47-48; and John 20:21. There is probably not a Christian in the world who hasn't heard of the Great Commission. I believe that very few Christians ever share their faith. That would mean that the vast majority of our congregations are in disobedience to the primary purpose of the church.

The lack of evangelism in our churches is not due to a lack of understanding the call to go. I believe that we want to obey, but there are other things that hinder us and keep us from fulfilling God's command to go. I believe the problems are fear, commitment, teaching, training, and the lack of a good strategy. If these elements are lacking, our witness will not be as effective. I find that most Christians don't have a problem with the Great Commission, they have a problem with who is to fulfill the Great Commission. Of course, the answer is the church. But if you were to probe a little deeper, you would find that most church members believe it is the job of the evangelist. The primary job of the evangelist, however, is not to win the lost. The primary job of the evangelist is to equip others in the Body to do evangelism (Eph. 4:10-13). People don't understand this.

For example, I get so excited about someone who has learned how to share Christ and is now excited about beginning to bring others to Christ. That is exciting and fulfilling to me. Why? The reason is my primary calling is to equip others. Now, God does use me to win souls to His kingdom; but to see someone else turned on to winning souls for Christ gives me a greater charge. There are a lot of people who have a true gift for soul winning. However, they may not equip others. The primary responsibility of the evangelist is to equip the Body with tools to effectively communicate the Gospel to others (Eph. 4:11-12).

If you were to look at 2 Corinthians 5:17-19, you would see that the responsibility to win the lost is given to all believers. That passage says, "Therefore if any man be in Christ, he is a new creature: old things are passed away; behold, all things are become new." I think that we can agree that this is referring to salvation. However, the next verse says that God has given to us, that is, the new Christian, a ministry—the ministry of reconciliation. God has given to all Christians a ministry to bring the lost man, woman, boy, and girl into a relationship with Himself.

Someone may say, "I don't know what to do! I don't know what to say!" In 2 Corinthians 5:19, God gives us two principles that can be used to win the lost without any formal training in evangelism. The two principles are (1) a word of reconciliation and (2) not pointing out the sins of the lost. All we need to do is to love the lost right where they are. If we would demonstrate God's love, then the person would know God loves him or her right where he or she is. This display of love alone would win the lost to Christ. We can clearly see from these Scriptures that it is the responsibility of each one of us to share Christ with a lost, confused, and dying world.

Fear, Commitment, and Deception

Fear and commitment are two key elements that keep us from evangelizing. All fear is not bad; however, when it stops us from what God has called us to do, then we know the fear is not from God. We must press past fear to get the job done. Fear can only be broken as we receive and act on God's word. His Word teaches us that the Holy Spirit and His Word will go before us to prepare our way and the heart of the unbeliever.

A person can learn everything there is to know about evangelism, but if he never leaves the four walls of the church, he will never break the fear and see the manifestation of the Spirit of God that has gone before him.

Fear and deception also effects our commitment. These are Satan's two biggest weapons against us. Fear and commitment are relationship problems. First John 4:18 says, "Perfected love casts out fear because fear involves torment" (NKJV). It's out of a consistent prayer life and fellowship in God's Word that the love of God is perfected in us. This will help us push past fear and bring us to a point of commitment.

Soul-Winning Evangelism Workshop

Prior to going out door-to-door, our members at Greenforest go through a two-hour Soul-Winning Evangelism Workshop. We know that knocking on doors is not the only method of evangelism, but the teaching and training in the workshop, the tally and the testimony have set our church on fire for evangelism. Comfort zones are being broken, fear is being broken, and the lost are being saved. Praise God! The evangelism seminar also equips us to do personal evangelism, as well as train a large number of persons at one time. The subjects taught place practical tools in the hands of members who have never witnessed before. Once they have completed the seminar, they are equipped to win the lost.

There are seven lessons taught in the Evangelism Workshop. Four of the lessons, entitled The State of the Lost, The Word of God at Work in the Lost, The Holy Spirit in the Life of the Lost, and The Witness of the Believer, come from the book *People Sharing Jesus,* by Darrell W. Robinson. The seminar topics are:

1. The State of the Unbeliever
2. God's Word at Work in the Lost
3. The Holy Spirit in the Life of the Lost
4. The Holy Spirit in the Life of the Witness
5. The Witness of the Believer
6. Tools in Our Hand
7. How to Share the Gospel

The State of the Unbeliever

The following Scriptures describe the condition the lost are in before receiving Christ. Once we know their state of being, it should place motivation within us to share Christ with them.

1. Under sin (Rom. 3:9)
2. Unrighteous (Rom. 3:10)
3. Guilty before God (Rom. 3:19)
4. Fallen short of God's glory (Rom. 3:23)
5. Enemies of God (Rom. 5:10)
6. Under a death sentence (Rom. 6:23)
7. Spiritually dead to the things of God (1 Cor. 2:14-16)
8. Blinded by Satan (2 Cor. 4:3-4)
9. Dead in trespasses and sin, walking according to demonic influences, fulfilling the desires of the flesh and mind, the children of wrath, uncircumcised heart, without Christ, aliens to the commonwealth of Israel, strangers to the covenants and promises of God, no hope, and without God in the world (Eph. 2).

God's Word at Work in the Life of the Lost

These are just a few Scriptures that indicate the importance of God's Word in the process of the new birth. God's Word cleanses us. The Word breaks up the hard heart, and is therefore able to be received. Faith comes by hearing the Word. Once the Word is received, God's power is released and a spiritual birth takes place.

1. God's Word cleans (Psalm 119:9)
2. God's Word breaks up our hard heart (Jer. 23:29)
3. God's Word is like a Sword (Eph. 6:17)
4. God's Word builds faith for salvation (Rom. 10:17; John 20:31)
5. God's Word is the power to save (Rom. 1:16)
6. We are born again by God's Word (1 Pet. 1:23)

We must be careful not to simply invite people to church. God's Word has to be part of the process. If we don't use God's Word, there will be no cleansing; faith will not be released for salvation; the power of God won't be present to save; and a spiritual birth will not take place. The Scripture teaches us that God confirms His Word with signs following (Mark 16:20). Our results will only be minimal without prayer and His Word.

The Holy Spirit's Role

The Holy Spirit is at work in the life of the lost person. He precedes the witness dealing with the lost person concerning the sin in his or her life, and revealing God's existence to him or her. The Holy Spirit also prepares the witness by empowering him or her to witness. He also gives us words to say and places those with receptive hearts in our life, so we can share Christ with them.

A. In the Life of the Lost
  1. Precedes the witness (Acts 9:10-12)

2. He convicts the world of sin (John 16:8)

3. He reveals God's existence (Rom. 1:18-23)

B. In the Believers' Life

1. Enables the believer (Acts 1:8)

2. Gives us boldness (Acts 4:30-31)

3. Helps our inadequacies (Luke 12:12)

C. Generates Divine Appointments (John 4:1-30; Acts 8:30; Acts 9:10-16)

The previous teaching illustrates what the Holy Spirit does to aid the believer, and the role the Holy Spirit plays in the life of the lost person. The testimonies from those in the Greenforest congregation confirm the work of the Holy Spirit. The Holy Spirit has given boldness and power, has spoken through persons, and has brought persons across our path who needed Christ. The Holy Spirit has brought us to a place where we knew it was nothing short of God's miraculous intervention and divine appointment.

The Witness of the Believer

God is holy, powerful, and sinless. The Holy Spirit is pure and gentle, yet God needs us to get the job done. Yes, as filthy as we are, He has allowed us to be laborers together with Him to win the lost. In Acts 8, God knew what the eunuch was reading. Yet he sent Philip to show him the way to salvation. In Acts 9, Jesus was talking directly to Paul. Yet, Jesus never told Paul how to be saved. Finally, in Acts 10, an angel spoke to

Cornelius. Yet, the divine visitations never yielded an explanation of God's plan of salvation. God has both commissioned and given the responsibility of communicating the Gospel to men (Matt. 10:1-15; 28:19; Mark 16:15). Without the witness of the believer, the message will never be shared. Moreover, the results will only yield more men bound for hell.

1. The Great Commission was given to men (Matt. 28:19; Mark 16:15).

2. Men testified of what they had both seen and heard (1 John 1:1-3).

3. Ethiopian eunuch stated, "How can I, except some man guide me" (Acts 8:30-31).

4. Cornelius was told, "A man will tell you what you should do" (Acts 10:1-6).

5. Paul was told what to do by a man (Acts 9:1-17).

Training

If we would be honest, there are a number of churches that hold evangelism seminars, but after the seminar is over, the spirit of evangelism begins to die. Teaching and preaching for the most part takes place in the sanctuary, or in a classroom setting. However, it has been my observation that to have an ongoing, effective evangelism ministry, training must always be a part of the equation. Training takes place in the field and guarantees the existence of the evangelism ministry beyond the teaching seminar. If we only have a seminar without providing an opportunity to practice what we have been taught in the classroom, the excitement will only last as long as the seminar itself. The workshop becomes just another evangelism seminar the members have attended. This problem occurs because there is not an implementation of what has been learned. Consequently, the spirit of evangelism will die in the congregation. Knowledge that is not acted upon will only leave people in bondage. Jesus said once we knew the truth, it would make us free (John 8:32). Jesus was talking about truth that liberates. When we act on God's Word and press past the fear that has us chained to our pews, then we will be free.

There are tremendous benefits that can be reaped when we experience in the field (neighborhoods) what we have learned in the classroom. How rewarding it is to be used by God to change someone's life. To be God's ear that hears, His voice that speaks, or His hand that touches. These benefits can only be experienced as we move from the pew to the streets and begin to witness to others. The benefits of leaving the pew and taking it to the streets are literally life changing, and include:

1. Breaking comfort zones
2. Breaking fear
3. Activating faith
4. Encouraging others
5. Producing a testimony
6. Giving experience
7. Opening the door to the gifts of the Spirit

Tally

Tally is accountability or record keeping. Members report the number of people who:

1. Had Christ shared with them.
2. Received Christ.
3. Are assured of their salvation.
4. Were restored to the faith.
5. Are enrolled in Sunday School.
6. Joined church.
7. Prayed for needs.

Testimony

After coming back from sharing Christ in the community, we spend time sharing what God has done. The testimony time is very exciting and will do two things in the congregation. First, the testimony will allow others who are full of apprehension to hear how God used someone as ordinary as himself or herself to change someone else's life. This will generate faith in others to be used by God in the same way. Second, as testimonies are shared in the congregation and witnesses spread the word about what God has done, others will come out and participate. I don't believe there should be just a small group, called "The Evangelism Team," but the whole church should win the lost. Testimonies will stir up the camp to create excitement and anticipation about a God that will do great exploits among His people.

Prayer, praise, worship and the four Ts—Teaching, Training, Tally, and Testimony—will produce tremendous results in our congregations. I would estimate that over 90 percent of the persons who have attended our workshop have never gone out before. Without exception, all of their testimonies have been immense. The excitement and the yokes that have been broken are tremendous. Members are saying how their comfort zones have been broken and how fulfilling the experience was to him or her. Plus, many stated all preconceived ideas were wrong concerning evangelism. The experience was nothing like they ever thought, and all their fears were dispelled. There is one lady in our church who was so full of fear that she would come to church after it began and would leave before service was over because she feared people. After going through the seminar, seven months later, she is still on fire and we can't keep her off the streets. Recently, one person began to cry in gratitude that God had broken the fear in her life. A minister shared with me, "I can preach to all of our members, but I was afraid to evangelize. Today God has broken the fear in my life." To God be all the glory. Testimonies will:

1. Encourage others.
2. Bring glory to God.
3. Help us to overcome fear.
4. Cause others to rejoice, too.
5. Release a spirit of evangelism in the church.

If the Fire Goes Out

If the fire of evangelism begins to go out, I want to give you five principles I practice to rekindle the flames again.

1. *Pray*—The very first problem may stem from a weak prayer life of the witness.
2. *Lead by example*—Leadership must set the tone. Lead your troops into battle and they will follow.
3. *Change your fishing spot* (Luke 5:1-7)—If the fish are not biting, change where you fish (evangelize).
4. *Give an opportunity to engage*—Always create the place and environment for evangelism. Make sure there is always what is known as "intentional evangelism." This is when you purposely go out to witness.
5. *Testify*—Allow testimonies about your evangelism efforts to be shared within the congregation. This, as we stated already, will ignite others in the congregation.

Chapter VIII Questions
Teaching, Tally, Testimony

1. Whose responsibility is it to share the Gospel?

   _____

   _____

2. To what ministry are we all called? Cite the Scripture reference.

   _____

   _____

3. What are the three commands Jesus gives in the Book of Matthew? Name the Scripture reference.

   1. _____
   2. _____
   3. _____

4. What is the primary job of the evangelist in Ephesians 4:11-13? _____

   _____

5. Name nine conditions of the lost.

   1. _____
   2. _____
   3. _____
   4. _____
   5. _____
   6. _____
   7. _____
   8. _____
   9. _____

6. Name six things the Word of God does in the life of the lost.

   1. _____
   2. _____
   3. _____
   4. _____
   5. _____
   6. _____

7. Explain why God's Word is important in the process of the new birth. _____
_____

_____
_____

8. What does the Holy Spirit do in the life of the lost person?

    1. _____
    2. _____
    3. _____
    4. _____

9. What does the Holy Spirit do in the life of the believer to prepare his or her way to witness?

    1. _____
    2. _____
    3. _____
    4. _____

10. List five Scripture references that support God's needing a witness.

    1. _____
    2. _____
    3. _____
    4. _____
    5. _____

11. List the seven benefits of training.

    1. _____
    2. _____
    3. _____
    4. _____
    5. _____
    6. _____
    7. _____

12. List seven areas that should be recorded (tallied).

    1. _____
    2. _____
    3. _____
    4. _____
    5. _____
    6. _____
    7. _____

13. What five benefits will the congregation reap from the testimony?

    1. _____
    2. _____
    3. _____

4. _____
5. _____

14. List five things you can do when the fire of evangelism dies.

    1. _____
    2. _____
    3. _____
    4. _____
    5. _____

CHAPTER IX
Tools in Our Hands
(For Sharing the Gospel)

There are five tools that I teach to be used to gather in the harvest. The tools are, *love* through the ministry of reconciliation, *personal testimony, invitation, excitement* and *prayer*.

Ministry of Reconciliation

Through love, the lost are drawn into God's kingdom. There are two principles found in 2 Corinthians 5:17-19 that can be used to win the lost without formal training: 1) not imputing their sin and 2) not pointing out their sins. (We are to love them right where they are, not condemn them to hell because of their sin.) The second principle is found in that same verse: "God has given us a word of reconciliation."

When a word spoken to a lost person is seasoned with salt, that word will give grace to the one who hears it (Col. 4:6). These principles work through the ministry of reconciliation, which God has given to all of us. These two principles alone could win the entire world to Christ.

Personal Testimony

Bo Mitchell, a great soul winner in God's kingdom, receives credit for what I have learned about our personal testimony. A testimony should consist of three parts: your life before Christ, your salvation experience, and your life since Christ has changed it. These three elements can be found in Paul's testimony to King Agrippa (Acts 26). Paul's testimony consisted of three parts. His life before Christ changed it, his conversion experience, and his life after he received Christ.

We should begin our testimony by asking the question, "May I share with you the most exciting thing that has ever happen in my life?" We should end the testimony by asking, "Has anything like this ever happened to you?" The person that argues Scriptures, can't dispute a strong testimony because it's factual.

Invitation

A good example of invitation can be found in John 1:35-51; 4:1-30, when Andrew came to his brother Peter and shared his experience of meeting Christ. The Scripture doesn't say he gave an invitation to Peter. However, I feel it's safe to assume he didn't pick Peter up and carry him to meet Jesus.

In verse 46, there is a conversation between Philip and Nathaniel. Philip gave an invitation to Nathaniel to "come and see," concerning Christ. These men knew each other. This teaches us that the kingdom of God is built on relationships.

In the story of the woman at the well, an invitation was given by the woman to "Come see a man!" (John 4:29). We must remember, however, that along with an invitation we must at some point present the Gospel. I know it is our purpose to invite someone to church so they can hear a message concerning salvation; however, what if they did not accept the invitation to come to church? The opportunity to share Christ to them may not come again.

Excitement

The nation of Israel had been looking for the Messiah for four hundred years. All they had was the word of the prophets, who said he would come. At this point, the kingdom of God had been literally held in prophecy. There had been others making the claim that they were the one who was to come as the Messiah. However, He had not yet come. What made the claim of Andrew and Philip so different from others making a claim to be the Messiah? What would make anyone leave his or her position to investigate a claim that, to this point, had gone unsubstantiated? The response to the invitation was based on the excitement within the invitation.

Another indication of this is the woman at the well in John 4. This woman was engaged in conversation with some of the same men she had slept with. What would make them investigate her claim to come see a man that, based on her report, was able to tell all things a person did. This would also mean the things they had been doing with her. Once again, I believe it was excitement. It was her excitement. Remember, she was living a life of obscurity. I can see her as she went from one place to the next conducting her business among people that had considered her a misfit because of her lifestyle. The time day she visited the well supports this. She didn't go down with the rest of the women in the community. Yet, the excitement she demonstrated before these men moved them to respond to her invitation. She was acting out of character, she was filled with excitement!

Prayer

Finally, we can use prayer as a tool to open a door to share the Gospel. In the Book of Acts 9:32-42, Peter prayed for two persons—the dead and the sick. God raised one from the dead and healed the other. The power of prayer is one of the tools in our hands, and it's a great tool to use. As I stated before, sometimes the only thing we can do is pray for a need that we can't physically meet before we can present the Gospel. Sometimes the need can only be met through prayer. Once we pray for the need then we can share Christ. Jesus always met the natural need first. This gave Him the right to speak to the person's life.

Once when our teams were in the field, there was a lady whose baby was sick. At the direction of the Holy Spirit, the team members went back to the lady's home and prayed for the baby. On Tuesday of the following week, the lady called the church and indicated that she hadn't had any trouble with her baby since her baby was prayed for. It was because of the prayer for the baby that the mother started coming to church. Prayer is a powerful tool.

Sharing the Gospel Message

While we should learn how to share the Gospel in some form, we need to be careful not to present something dry or something that sounds like it's read. The message should be inviting, giving hope, causing a desire to respond—even if the response is negative. I just tell the Gospel story using Scriptures without citing chapter and verse, except Romans 10:9-10. Even the teen presentation is done in story form, quoting the verses without Scripture references.

The Gospel Message Should Consist of Five Points:
1. God's purpose

    A. A better life now (John 10:10)

    B. An eternal life (John 3:16)
2. Our sin nature

    A. Sin keeps us from what God has for us (Ps. 51:5)

    B. The sin of Adam was passed on to all men (Rom. 5:12)

    C. All have sinned (Rom. 3:23)

    D. Sin must be judged (Rom. 6:23)
3. Repent and come by faith alone

A. God commands all men to repent (Acts 17:30)

B. Repent and be converted (Acts 3:19)

C. Saved by grace through faith, not works (Eph. 1:8-9)

4. Accept God's plan through Jesus Christ

    A. God came in the flesh in the person of Jesus (John 1:1, 14)

    B. Christ suffered for our sin (1 Pet. 3:8)

    C. God has laid our sin on Jesus (Is. 53:6)

5. Surrender our life and receive Christ

    A. Believe He gives us the power to become His son or daughter (John 1:12)

    B. Believe in your heart and make confession with your mouth (Rom. 10:9-10)

    C. Pray with the person to receive Christ

    D. Unite ourselves with Him in baptism (Rom. 6:4)

Another way to share the Gospel is based on Ezekiel 23:30. In this Scripture, God looked for a man to stand in the middle of the hedge that was broken. The hedge was broken because of sin. This can be used to illustrate man's broken relationship with God. With God on one side of the hedge, man on the other, and sin in the middle, we can illustrate how Jesus restored our broken relationship with God.

Three Most Common Answers

There are three common responses people will give:

1. I've been a good person
2. I've been baptized
3. I'm a church member

While all of these are good, none of them will save you. One must be born again (John 3:7), which means to be born from above. Romans 4 and Ephesians 2 clearly teach us that works alone can never guarantee our salvation. Faith stands alone as the only way to receive salvation.

Encourage the New Converts
1. To attend church regularly.
2. To read the Bible daily (beginning with the Book of John, which shows the deity of Jesus).
3. To pray daily, developing a personal relationship with Jesus.
4. To share Christ with others. If the new Christian imitates what he or she sees other church members doing, and if we do not witness and lead by example, the new convert will do similarly.

Instructions Before Going Out to the Community
1. Determine the targeted group and location to be evangelized.
2. Divide team members into groups of two or three. For a team of two, one should witness while the other person prays and records information. If the

team has three members one should witness, one pray, and the other person record information.

3. Prepare maps indicating the route to the location to be evangelized and street or apartments to be worked.

4. Bring documentation forms to record information. These forms should record the name, address, phone number, and their response after sharing the Gospel.

5. Carry tracts and church brochures—these are always important items to take when evangelizing. A tract and church brochure serve as a way to continue witnessing long after you have left the residence. With the name and address of the church, the lost person will be able to contact or come by the church at some point in the future.

6. Determine the mode of transportation—Will individual team members drive, or should one vehicle transport the entire team? This is important because too many vehicles could cause traffic problems or hinder residents from parking.

7. Pray for forgiveness, sin may be in the camp.

In Joshua 7, Israel didn't attain victory because "sin was in the camp." We need to ask God for forgiveness before we engage in battle with the enemy. If not, we may experience the same results Israel did when they tried to face their enemy while sin was in the camp. The only result will be defeat.

The following pages will give examples of materials we use to record information.

```
┌─────────────────────────────────────────────────┐
│                WITNESSING LOG                   │
│  Name _____  │
│  Address _____  │
│  _____   │
│  Phone _____  │
│  E-mail _____  │
│  Shared Christ ____      Received Christ ____   │
│  Assured of Salvation ____  Restored to Christ ____ │
│  Enrolled in Sunday School ____  Prayed for needs ____ │
│  Comments _____  │
│  _____   │
│  Please Sign _____  │
│  Date _____         │
└─────────────────────────────────────────────────┘
```

The witnessing log records the resident who is not at home.

Melvin Haynes, a member of Greenforest, suggests a very effective approach to be used at the door to open a conversation.

Hello, my name is _____ from _____ Church. We are (1) in the area meeting our neighbors; (2) sharing information concerning our church; and (3) assuring them of their salvation.

At this point:
1. Share the information.
2. Assure them of their salvation, at which time other needs surface.

To make the transition into the Gospel, ask this question: "Have you come to the place in your life that you know for certain you have eternal life and if you were to die, you would go to heaven?"

Second question after response: "If you were standing before God right now, and He asked "Why should I let you into My heaven?" what would you say?"

These two questions come from the CWT Evangelism Program used by the Southern Baptist Convention, and are excellent.

```
Name _____

Address _____

        _____

Phone   _____
   Response:
Shared Christ _____    Enrolled in Sunday School _____
Received Christ _____          Prayed for needs _____
Assured of Salvation _____        Joined church _____
Restored to Christ _____
```

Chapter IX Questions

Evangelism Tools

1. Name five evangelism tools in our hands.

    1. _____
    2. _____
    3. _____
    4. _____
    5. _____

2. Name the five points of the Gospel presentation.

    1. _____
    2. _____
    3. _____
    4. _____
    5. _____

3. Name the three most common answers after sharing the Gospel.

   1. _____
   2. _____
   3. _____

4. Before going out into the community we should prepare. List seven things we should do to prepare.

   1. _____
   2. _____
   3. _____
   4. _____
   5. _____
   6. _____
   7. _____

Chapter X
The Delivery System

The vehicle is the method used to carry the Gospel to the residents in the community. Sunday School has been around for hundreds of years and serves as the greatest vehicle to funnel ministry. The Fivefold Ministry Purposes of the Church (evangelism, fellowship, discipleship, missions, and ministry) discussed earlier are what Greenforest Community Baptist Church uses within their Sunday School to cause effective ministry within the congregation and in the community.

The Sunday School can be used as a mighty force of ministry! There are a number of reasons for using the Sunday School as a vehicle for ministry:

1. The Sunday School has been proven throughout history to be the most effective vehicle to evangelize.
2. It has the second largest number of members who meet through the week, which allows a larger group of persons to be involved in ministry.
3. It has discipleship already in place.
4. Leadership is already in place.

5. When evangelism is done through the classes, enrollment can be done.

6. It creates small groups.

7. Personal needs are met in a small group setting.

8. It creates a warm market for evangelism.

9. All who are evangelized can be placed in their own age groups.

10. Evangelism can be done in small groups in the members' neighborhoods.

11. It gives the members a place to develop their spiritual gifts.

12. It creates a safe place for nonbelievers to learn about Christ and build relationships.

Sunday School in a Changing World

We are living in changing times, and while we don't change the Gospel, we may need to revisit our methods of implementation. In the case of members who have not shown an interest in Sunday School regardless of all our efforts, I would like to make some suggestions:

1. Satellite Sunday School classes
2. Parking lot Sunday School
3. Correspondence Sunday School
4. E-mail Sunday School
5. Be open to change

Satellite Sunday School Class

The satellite class is designed to meet the needs of lost persons in our neighborhoods who don't attend church nor want to attend church. Their reasons may vary, but may be valid. This is an effort to reach the lost by inviting them to a nonthreatening environment. By this we mean that we invite them to a Sunday School class in their own neighborhood, where they may feel more comfortable. This needs to be a relaxed environment where they can come in casual clothing and enjoy the company of neighbors. The setting is one where they can get their questions answered and receive prayer for their needs. The atmosphere is very cordial. The satellite class can be used to bridge the lost person into church or to plant a new church in the area. My suggestion is to hold the satellite class on Saturday evening or Sunday morning; however, it can be held at any time.

The satellite classes can be formed after members have evangelized their neighborhood or before evangelism has taken place. If evangelism is done first, an invitation will be given at the door to attend a neighborhood fellowship where their questions can be answered concerning life problems and answers can be discussed based on biblical principles. I think we need to be up front with our neighbors and tell them what we're doing. Let them know this is a place where they can receive prayer, get questions answered and their needs met, but the answers will come from God's Word. My suggestion is that you concentrate on one street at a time, making sure each home has had a visitation. Flyers can be distributed inviting neighbors over to a member's home for fellowship and Bible study. This can be an effective way to reach our lost neighbors. It was through the breaking of bread from house to house that the church experienced tremendous growth (Acts 2:42-47).

God wants us to get out from beyond the church walls and reach out to a world that needs love. The satellite strategy is a comfortable way to reach those around us in a non-threatening way, bringing them into an environment that will meet their needs and expose them to the God that they have heard about but may not have experienced in a real way. The satellite class can also serve as the vehicle to attract the lost to the church. In most cases we're trying to get the lost to come to our churches when we need to go to them. It may be wiser to keep them in their own environment or cultural setting, where they will feel more comfortable. We have to remember that for them to leave from where they are and come to our churches, it may be a culture shock to them. This is the reason why we need to leave the four walls and go to the lost in their communities. The satellite class meets a need that is produced by a changing society.

Two of the biggest problems the church will face in the twenty-first century will be meeting the needs of people and ascertaining how to gather in the harvest. I believe the satellite strategy will address both of these problems through small groups, as we reach out in our communities. The neighborhood satellite Sunday School class can be used to meet needs, build a bridge to the church, or to plant a church in that community. Once one street has been evangelized and needs have been met, the strategy can be duplicated on subsequent streets, evangelizing and fulfilling the fivefold ministry purposes. A satellite class can be in every neighborhood, or persons can be directed to one within a two-mile radius from their home. In the case of an apartment community, I feel it would be better to have the class on site. There is a whole community living within an apartment complex. This strategy will meet the needs we face in the twenty-first century.

Parking Lot Sunday School

This strategy is used to catch members driving away. The teachers can set up a booth with some refreshments to attract the fleeing members. As they stop by the table to dine, they can be asked to join the class already in session on the grounds near the booth. Once they stop by and take the food, it's like having a fish on the line—just pull him in; hence, parking lot Sunday School.

Correspondence Sunday School

This strategy is developed for members who will not attend regardless of what you do. My suggestion is to give them a lesson and some questions to complete at home. They would complete and return the lesson the next week. Hence, we have correspondence Sunday School. It's my hope that by completing lessons at home, a desire will develop to attend a regular class at church. As long as you have a name, address, and phone number, you have a member. Correspondence Sunday School may be the best vehicle to catch the fleeing member.

E-mail Sunday School

In a computer society, e-mail Sunday School can be another way to educate our members in God's Word. Correspondence can be sent to persons over the information superhighway. They can receive a lesson, with questions, and answer back through e-mail. We're not suggesting that assembling for worship be forsaken; we can't, God's Word commands it. However, Sunday School is not in the Bible. The concept of Sunday School was started a few hundred years ago, so the method of delivery can be changed.

Open to Change

We have members who would love to attend Sunday School; however, they are unable because of their job schedule. We need to keep ourselves open to innovative ideas that the Holy Spirit may give us. One option would be to offer Sunday School on some other day of the week, as well as Sunday.

When we look at God's Word, God had people do some strange things. Naaman had to dip in the muddy water. Moses put a branch in the water to heal its bitterness. Jesus even made spittle and put in on a man's eyes. Yes, God has chosen foolish things to advance the Gospel. We must always be open and willing to change our methods and our strategies, but the Gospel should never be changed. When something doesn't consistently work for you, you need to make a change. In Luke 5, the disciples had fished all night but caught nothing. On the suggestion of Jesus, they made a little adjustment and caught so many fish they needed help pulling them in.

Maybe we need to change our strategy. Be open to hear God's voice and be willing to change. Old methods seem to die hard, but results are what we're after. God knows how to gather the harvest, and He knows the best method to use. He knows where to tell us to drop the net to catch the greatest harvest. Be open to change.

Chapter X Questions

The Delivery System

1. The Sunday School serves as the greatest vehicle to do effective ministry. List twelve reasons to support this statement.

   1. _____
   2. _____
   3. _____
   4. _____
   5. _____
   6. _____
   7. _____
   8. _____
   9. _____
   10. _____
   11. _____
   12. _____

2. List five ways to revolutionize Sunday School in a changing world.

   1. _____
   2. _____
   3. _____
   4. _____
   5. _____

3. Can you think of other ways to revitalize Sunday School?

   _____
   _____

Chapter XI

Rewards of the Labor

God has promised benefits to those who work in the field of harvest. If you think about it, there are four things employers provide for their employees:

1. A place to work
2. Tools to do the job
3. A paycheck
4. Benefits

The Workplace

God's workplace is the "Field of Harvest." We don't need directions to find it. In fact, it's all around us. The field is the neighborhood you live in. It's the place you work, your town, city, state, country, and the world. The field, or God's place of employment, is any place where the people are. The workplace is the field, and the field is people. The only question is, Do we want to be employed? There are a lot of "help wanted" signs on the faces of those who come in and out of our lives on a daily basis.

Did you see the help wanted sign on the television set the last time you watched? What about the people you work with or those who live in your neighborhood? Yes, millions of faces across the world stare back at us daily saying "help wanted." Some of us were hired, we took the job, but we haven't shown up for work yet. In other words, we received salvation; however, salvation is just the requirement to work in the field. Maybe some of us missed that during the orientation process.

Being saved means more than heaven. It's a life of service and sharing the Good News that Jesus came to make a real difference in your life. It's our job to tell them. Most of the jobs I have had in my life came by someone sharing the good news: "They're hiring over there." We don't mind sharing good news with our friends about employment, but what about Jesus and the power He makes available to us to change our life? What about His power to forgive our sin? Why don't we share that? The fields are ripe for harvest, and the highways and hedges are, too (John 4:35, Luke 14:23). Let us not just take the job (a ticket to heaven), but let us show up for work and enter into the field of harvest.

Tools

Tools were discussed in chapter seven. However, tools are anything we use to share the Gospel. You may use your testimony as a tool to win someone to Christ. It may be through the tool of prayer or invitation that someone receives Jesus. Maybe God will use your excitement to draw someone to Himself. It doesn't really matter what tool you use, just use one. You'll feel good after a good day's work.

Pay and Benefits

The Scripture states that God loads us with benefits daily (Ps. 68:19). The following list reveals other benefits for those who labor. The soul winner:

1. Receives wisdom (Prov. 11:30).

2. Shines bright (Dan. 12:3; Prov. 4:18; Matt. 13:43).

3. Receives joy over their fruit both on earth and in heaven (Ps. 126:6; Luke 15:6-7).

4. Receives wages and gathers fruit (John 4:36).

5. Causes others to rejoice (Acts 15:3).

6. Saves a soul from death (James 5:20).

7. Receives a crown of life (1 Thess. 2:19).

These are the rewards that we can expect for being employed by God. I am sure we all can bear witness to God loading us daily with benefits.

The benefits that we receive are not just tangible in nature. Some of the things we struggle with on a daily basis will become less significant, or the need will be met once we begin to witness and minister to others. God has designed it that way. You meet someone's need and God will meet your need.

Chapter XI Questions

Labor and Reward

Name seven rewards of laboring in the fields of harvest, and list the Scripture references.

1. _____
2. _____
3. _____
4. _____
5. _____
6. _____
7. _____

Conclusion

I trust and pray that this book has been a blessing to you. I pray that for those who need help in the area of evangelism, the information contained within the pages of this book will equip you to become more skilled in your witness for Christ. I also pray that you will enter the harvest field and begin to reap the harvest, and that God begins to load you with additional benefits. Then will God receive the glory as His kingdom expands on the earth.

To God is all the glory. Amen!

About the Author

The Reverend David W. Hopewell, Sr. is Minister of Evangelism at Greenforest Community Baptist Church in Decatur, Georgia, and founder of The Joshua Evangelism Ministry. Rev. Hopewell has spent the past twenty-four years helping pastors in the area of church growth and evangelism. He also has helped to plant five churches, two of which he pastored.

Rev. Hopewell has a passion for lost persons, but he has a greater passion for equipping the body of Christ to reach the lost. He is an evangelism strategist, organizer, motivational and seminar speaker. Rev. Hopewell's wife and four children also help and support him in ministry.

www.ingramcontent.com/pod-product-compliance
Lightning Source LLC
LaVergne TN
LVHW011424080426
835512LV00005B/250

*9 7 8 1 8 9 1 7 7 3 3 0 3 *